THE
COMPLETE GUIDE
TO
NONTRADITIONAL
EDUCATION

THE COMPLETE GUIDE TO NONTRADITIONAL EDUCATION

William J. Halterman

Facts On File
New York

Published by Facts on File, Inc.
460 Park Avenue South, New York, N.Y. 10016

Library of Congress Cataloging in Publication Data

Halterman, William J.
  Complete guide to non-traditional education.

  Includes index.
    1. Nonformal education—United States—Directories.
2. Correspondence schools and courses—United States—
Directories.   3. Nonformal education—Directories.
4. Correspondence schools and courses—Directories.
I. Title.
L901.H27   1983   374′.4′02573   82-12105
  ISBN 0-87196-796-0 (pbk)
  ISBN 0-87196-798-7 (HC)

10 9 8 7 6 5 4 3 2 1
Printed in the United States of America

CONTENTS

PREFACE

WHAT IS NONTRADITIONAL EDUCATION?

The term *nontraditional education* comprises a number of different elements such as, but not limited to, the following: the awarding of academic credit for experiential learning; correspondence study that is self-paced; using the world as one's classroom and instructor; the awarding of academic credit simply by examination. In fact, it is not easy to define a field as philosophically broad as nontraditional education.

Title 1 of the Higher Education Act of 1965, Section 132, defines nontraditional or lifelong learning as follows:

> Lifelong learning includes, but is not limited to, adult basic education, continuing education, independent study, agricultural education, business education and labor education, occupational education and job training programs, parent education, postsecondary education, preretirement and education for older and retired people, remedial education, special education for groups or for individuals with special needs, and also educational activities designed to upgrade occupational and professional skills, to assist business, public agencies, and other organizations in the use of innovation and research results, and to serve family needs and personal development.

The legislative assistant who drafted this legislation was obviously being certain to cover all bases and possibilities.

Yet nontraditional education can frequently be a faster means of achieving a legitimate college-level degree, providing the individual is sincerely motivated. Moreover, the impetus to lifelong learning has been accelerated in recent years by numerous factors varying from a need to keep job skills from becoming obsolescent, to a desire to keep abreast of our changing times, to a search for personal fulfillment.

Nontraditional education is for you if . . .
- **You seek a flexible education designed for your needs.**
- **You are employed or have other full-time pursuits and cannot participate in a traditional on-campus program.**
- **You have "experiential" learning that can be translated into college credits.**
- **You are interested in further education to pass a certification test.**

Many individuals do not have the time to attend traditional programs that require extensive physical contact with the campus, professor, and other students. It is for this reason that THE COMPLETE GUIDE TO NONTRADITIONAL EDUCATION devotes considerable attention to nontraditional, self-paced, "correspondence" institutions. Many of the institutions assessed in this book award college credits after analyzing your experiential learning and educational background, with no additional requirements.

THE
COMPLETE GUIDE
TO
NONTRADITIONAL
EDUCATION

1
INTRODUCTION

There are innumerable guides to traditional education available at bookstores or your local library. THE COMPLETE GUIDE TO NONTRADITIONAL EDUCATION is basically designed for the mid-career adult professional confronted with the reality that an advanced degree is required if he or she is to advance in a career. A major failing of traditional guides to traditional universities is that even when those institutions have alternative, correspondence, or nontraditional education available to lifelong learners, little or no mention is made of such programs. This guide has been prepared to help solve this unfortunate case of benign neglect. It will provide you with the current information based on an on-going survey of nontraditional educational programs around the country. To date, programs in forty states and the District of Columbia are included.

While a degree—any degree—is useful, it is worth remembering that the type of degree and the transcript of the student's work are generally more important to an employer than the name of the university or college awarding it. If an employer is seeking a college graduate with certain skills (e.g., accounting), that employer will examine the transcript and not merely take any college graduate. The fact also remains that if the employer has a choice between a college graduate and a nongraduate, the graduate tends to be hired, at least for jobs above a certain level.

It is important to be judicious in applying for admission to any specific program. Simple admission to nontraditional or correspondence programs is not where difficulty arises for the adult interested in lifelong learning. How many of your previous college credits will count? How much, if any, credit is given for experiential learning? Will you be required to take a large number of courses, even if they are self-paced? Will some personal contact be required with the campus? These are only a few of the important questions which the potential student must resolve before enrolling in any nontraditional program. If your needs and future career and personal goals are not thoroughly thought through, the possibilities for wasting time, effort, and money rise dramatically.

There are still academics who have a haughty disdain for the concept of nontraditional education and the degrees that are awarded, whether they teach at a proprietary institution or a state-funded school. There have always been academic conservatives whose undying belief has been that the modern age has diluted the purity and value of academic credentials. Clearly, in an ideal world people would rise on the basis of their abilities and willingness to work, but we are still some distance from utopia.

In 1979 the president of New York University criticized nontraditional education, stating that "Higher education is approaching the territory of lifelong learning with standards, forethought, and a sense of dignity reminiscent of the California Gold Rush." Concerns for the "dignity" of acacemics aside, such criticism is premised on the idea that the traditional educational system came down in final form from the Mount with Moses and that education does not change over time to serve different populations. Another professor went so far as to state that the nontraditional student is in a much better position to learn and is more likely to do so, when compared to the person in the traditional classroom who may neither be as motivated nor receive much individual attention from the instructor.

Fortunately, not all traditional academics are so critical of new approaches to

3

education, and there has generally been increasing support for, and interest in, such approaches. The Carnegie Commission on Nontraditional Study estimated that there were thirteen million adults involved in "noncollegiate education" in 1973. According to a survey conducted by the National Home Study Council on correspondence students, the average age of such students is now 35, 84 percent are high school graduates, and more than half have annual incomes in excess of $10,000. According to the Census Bureau, students taking fewer than 12 semester hours of credit are now a majority in postsecondary education.

Traditional academics may oppose such educational innovations, yet these adaptations of the traditional system were preordained by a declining birth rate and the overall aging of the population. The concept of education as something acquired once when young and then lasting a lifetime is outdated and has been discarded by all who recognize the constant need to adapt as the way to survival in an increasingly complex world.

In *The Carnegie Commission on Nontraditional Study: Diversity by Design* defined nontraditional study in the following manner:

> It is an attitude that puts the student first and the institution second, concentrates more on the former's need than the latter's convenience, encourages diversity of individual opportunity rather than uniform prescription, and deemphasizes time, space, and even course requirements in favor of competence, for the degree learner of any age and circumstance, for the degree aspirant as well as the person who finds sufficient reward in enriching life through constant, periodic, or occasional study. This attitude is not new; it is simply more prevalent than it used to be. (San Francisco: Jossey-Bass, 1973, p. xv)

It also is a fact that colleges are desperate for enrollments in these times of constricted Federal and state budgets. Nontraditional courses are money-makers, a situation recognized by a number of very traditional universities and colleges. Such institutions have never hesitated to hand out honorary doctorates to wealthy donors and celebrities who might attract donations to the school. The truth is that the demands of the free marketplace have begun to affect the lives of academics, and many resent the situation.

We all recognize that very little often distinguishes people working the same job—*except* that the person with a college education is likely to advance much faster, earn more, have higher prestige, and enjoy a host of other benefits.

A survey published by a leading university in the nontraditional-education field notes that half of their graduates "received a salary increase or a more prestigious position as a result of their degree." Another survey, of United Auto Workers and Steelworkers by the University of Michigan, showed about sixty percent interested in further off-campus/ nontraditional education. They were specifically interested in courses that were job-related, such as mathematics, computer science, industrial engineering, or leadership development. The implications of these two surveys are clear.

This book cannot overemphasize the fact that a degree is a degree is a degree, *providing* that it is awarded by a reputable institution. At a job interview it is only rarely that anything more than superficial questions are asked about one's formal educational background. For one thing, most of us do not go into the area of major concentration we studied in college but, instead, are blown about by the winds of fate. One major strength of the nontraditional approach is that the student quite frequently has work experience in his or her field of study. This observer does not view the awarding of credit for such experience as "meaningless" devaluation of academic standards. The time has long past for academics to fully recognize that mid-career professional people with family responsibilities cannot, and are not willing to, spend their evenings and weekends cloistered on ivy-covered campuses with professors—too many of whom know less much about their subject than the student working in the field.

The fact is that after five years on the same job, there is no difference between a college graduate and a nongraduate, *except* in the paths their careers are likely to follow. Studies have shown time and again that college graduates earn more over a lifetime than those who do not attend or graduate from college. The central fact remains that while there is no real difference in the levels of working knowledge between college graduates and noncollege graduates, a degree is the ticket frequently required for career success by a society that often demands credentials rather than takes the time to recognize talent and intelligence in an individual.

Unquestionably, there are those who disapprove of nontraditional education because they feel that such degrees are too easy to attain. But while no reasonable person would condone 'diploma mills," it is absurd to condemn nontraditional or continuing education for adults that allows them to undertake serious study part-time, at home, evenings, or weekends and provides academic credit for what they already know. Acquaintance with the ideas of Plato or Bertrand Russell notwithstanding, it is doubtful that the disapproval of academic conservatives is of earth-shattering importance to the vast majority of sensible individuals whose identity does not depend upon having endured a certain number of years of classroom drill. It must be remembered that degrees do not confer wisdom nor knowledge, they are merely the outward sign recognized by society for individual accomplishment.

Education is a commodity. Indeed, it is such a commodity that many colleges and university communities are vigorously selling themselves today as a direct consequence of shrinking enrollments (alas, for academics, the end of the "baby boom") and constricted funding.

The degree fetish that this country has developed is unhealthy for our society. A genuine respect for talent, intelligence, and knowledge is frequently difficult to find, even though the American system is far more open than many others around the world. Fortunately, the United States has not yet gone to the extremes of a class-conscious country such as Great Britain, where upward mobility is much more restricted than here. The degree mania present in our society today is concerned with learning and competence to be sure, but it is also often seen as another hurdle to jump in the endless race to get ahead.

Credit for courses previously completed must be carefully evaluated by a reputable institution to ascertain whether it is applicable to the program and degree you seek. If you have participated in courses or programs, seminars or workshops, if you have expe-

5

rience gained from military, business, or government affiliations or service—all these must be carefully evaluated to insure that the proper amount of credit is awarded. Any institution that is overly generous with such college credits for life experience should be viewed with a degree of skepticism.

Most nontraditional programs are based upon a core of knowledge in three primary areas: humanities, the natural sciences, and the social sciences. You may have life experiences which can be partially credited toward the fulfillment of these basic requirements. You may also obtain credit through satisfactory completion of general examinations, such as the College Level Examination Program.

At this juncture the point must be made that those without previous college education or experience of some other formal study will not likely do well starting from scratch in a self-paced, nontraditional type of program. The promotional literature of Syracuse University estimates that it "will take seven years for you to complete the 120 semester hours" required for one of its degrees if you have no prior credits. There are, of course, legitimate nontraditional programs that take considerably less time than this, but they are likely to be offered by private, proprietary institutions.

Many mid-career people rightly feel they deserve to receive academic credit for what they have learned in the "school of hard knocks," a fact that is taken into account by this publication. Unless you take advantage by "attending" an institution offering college credits for experiential learning, a college program may simply be too long. For most of us, there are already not enough hours in the day, without the problem of making a long-term commitment of precious time to an educational program.

Nonetheless, simply because a program is nontraditional does not automatically mean that it will offer credits for experiential learning, nor should one assume that these degrees are easy to attain, because such is definitely not the case. In many instances nontraditional degrees can be more difficult to attain than those from traditional universities. Among the schools listed in this book Walden, Heed, and Nova are institutions, for example, with rigorous standards for the Ph.D. degree, compared with the same degree offered by traditional universities.

The would-be nontraditional student must remember that many independent-degree programs limit your options for study. The Lifelong Learning promotional literature of Ohio University states: "It is possible to receive a degree exclusively through courses offered in the independent degree program, although this limits your choice of courses and degree programs." Ohio University is a traditional school with nontraditional/correspondence offerings, which accounts for the limitations. Institutions more clearly nontraditional in character, where the student is involved in establishing his course of study, offer greater flexibility than traditional institutions with some correspondence or external study programs.

One final question you should resolve prior to undertaking any given educational program is whether it is the one that will lead to your ultimate goal. Always make certain that any credential you are aiming to receive at the conclusion of your studies is acceptable for certification purposes by your employer or prospective employer. There could be a major disappointment awaiting you if you don't ask this question first.

2

CREDIBILITY, ACCREDITATION, AND DIPLOMA MILLS

One may view accreditation (the means by which colleges, universities, and other school programs are certified) in many ways. Some view accreditation as vitally necessary to protect the quality of education from the open assault of charlatans and hucksters. Others tend to view accreditation as the part of the educational system that succeeds in stifling education rather than promoting it, in the belief that learning and the appreciation of knowledge are what education is supposed to be about rather than worrying about what outside examiners may think.

The credibility of an institution is an issue separate from its accreditation and the legal status. California, for example, has a law which allows for the creation of private ("proprietary") institutions that are legally authorized to award college degrees, but such institutions may not be accredited by the regional authority. (There has been some controversy in recent years about who accredits the accreditors and by what criteria they do so, but these arguments are not germane and are too arcane for our interests herein.)

A degree may be awarded by an accredited institution, but there is a definite pecking-order among the institutions of higher education. Too many people now survive an education rather than have one that becomes central to their way of life. It has become important to choose an educational program intelligently rather than assume they offer equal value.

Accreditation of colleges and universities, whether traditional or nontraditional, as well as practically any training school or program, is an area where there are no national standards. As noted by a publication from the Office of Post-secondary Education at the Department of Education:

> The United States has no Federal Ministry of education or other centralized authority exercising single national control over educational institutions in this country. The States assume varying degrees of control over education, but, in general, institutions of postsecondary education are permitted to operate with considerable independence and autonomy. As a consequence, American educational institutions can vary widely in the character and quality of their programs.
>
> In order to insure a basic level of quality, the practice of accreditation arose in the United States as a means of conducting nongovernmental, peer evaluation of educational institutions and programs. Private educational associations of regional or national scope have adopted criteria reflecting the qualities of a sound educational program and have developed procedures for evaluating institutions or programs to determine whether or not they are operating at basic levels of quality.

A good rule of thumb in assessing the credibility of a nontraditional program is that the faster the degree comes, and the more eager the institution is to enroll the student, the more likely that it is worthless.

Simply because a degree is offered in a nontraditional fashion does not automatically mean that your experiential learning and college credits will add up to an instant degree. We cannot overemphasize the fact that a fraudulent degree from a diploma mill is worse than having no degree whatsoever.

9

Phrases in the literature of diploma mills such as "no-cost evaluation," or an appeal for you to "earn" your degree now by sending the enrollment form—and the appropriate "tuition" fee—are warnings about the probable illegitimacy of the "institution" in question. If it operates out of a post-office box and you cannot locate a campus or very respectable set of offices, do not spend your money. Be wary of those institutions whose faculty has graduated from that institution or from foreign institutions you have never heard of. We have checked the institutions included in THE COMPLETE GUIDE TO NONTRADITIONAL EDUCATION by making inquiries to them under a number of different names, from different states, and in some instances, through telephone calls. There is every reason to believe that no diploma mills have slipped past. Anyone experiencing difficulty with any institution included herein, or who has discovered a new and interesting program, is invited to contact the compiler of this work, through the publisher.

Accreditation is not the same as credibility, a fact which deserves emphasis. *Lovejoy's College Guide* has the following to say about accreditation:

> Senior institutions which do not have accreditation by one of the six regional bodies but . . . may have approval or recognition by their state universities, state boards or departments of education. Some of these colleges may have had regional accreditation in past years but lost it because of one weakness or another. Some, conceivably, might have obtained regional accreditation but elected not to seek it. Some are among the nation's oldest colleges, some are commendable new institutions, while others are not impressive because of their limited facilities.

The credibility and acceptability of the nontraditional institution for the adult learner will be of far greater concern than whether it meets criteria such as having enough books in its library—or having a library at all, for that matter.

The National Home Study Council, founded in 1926, sponsors an independent nine-member Accrediting Commission. Shortly after its founding in 1955, the U.S. Office of Education recognized this organization as a "nationally recognized accrediting agency," which currently accredits ninety home-study schools. Private and correspondence institutions may apply for accreditation. The NHSC is the only organization listed by the Department of Education which accredits home-study schools. Very few proprietary schools offer college credit, although California is among the leaders in this field because of a progressive state law which encourages diversity in education, thereby recognizing that the government ought not have a monopoly or absolute franchise-granting power over who may operate an institution of learning. (See Appendix C)

The reader must bear in mind that one can spend years delving into any one aspect of the various elements of the subject of accreditation. The user of nontraditional education will have to be the ultimate judge of the effectiveness of the program he or she chooses.

Each student will have different goals, varying life experiences, educational backgrounds, and interests that differ. Some will not want to spend much time getting a credential for what they already know, while others will be willing to study for a lengthy period of time. Indeed, some of you may choose to earn more than one degree, possibly from differing institutions, for personal reasons, career purposes, economic reasons, or simply to make certain that all educational bases are covered.

It is worth remembering that education does not cost, it pays! You will find, particularly as a mature, mid-career professional, that the costs of education are insignificant when weighed against its real and intangible benefits. Nonetheless, you may take certain educational costs as a tax write-off, under the following criteria: first, you must pursue the education to maintain or improve skills required in business or employment; second, you may deduct the cost of education if it is expressly required by your employer; finally, if you are taking further education to meet the requirements of a set of regulations, laws, or for professional certification, etc., then the expense is also likely to be deductible.

The applicable regulation from the Internal Revenue Service code is as follows:

1. 162-5 EXPENSES FOR EDUCATION

(a) *General Rule.* Expenditures made by an individual for education, including research undertaken as part of his educational program (with certain exceptions), are deductible as ordinary and necessary business expenses (even though the education may lead to a degree) if the education—

(1) Maintains or improves skills required by the individual in his employment or other trade or business, or

(2) Meets the express requirements of the individual's employer, or the requirements of applicable law or regulations, imposed as a condition to the retention by the individual of an established employment relationship, status, or rate of compensation.

3

DEPARTMENT OF DEFENSE AND VETERANS ADMINISTRATION PROGRAMS

Veterans are eligible for educational benefits under two programs. The Veterans Readjustment Benefits Act of 1966 (the so-called GI Bill) covers those who served between February 1, 1955, and December 31, 1976. Individuals who served honorably 18 months or more on active duty are eligible for up to the equivalent of 45 months of full-time schooling or on-job training. Educational assistance for service personnel who served after January 1, 1977, is based upon a contributory plan. Most military members have ten years after separation from the service or, depending on circumstances, until December 31, 1989, to utilize their benefits. Checking with your local Veterans Administration office will provide more specific information.

Under the Veterans Readjustment Benefits Act of 1966, the veteran is entitled to 1½ months of educational assistance for each month actually served. Certain children and spouses are also eligible for benefits if the service member died of service-connected causes or if they have a permanent service-connected disability.

Veterans entering college must submit the form known as VA 22-1990, along with necessary supporting documents. Veterans who have attended another college and drawn VA benefits must submit form VA 22-1995. This form lists the names and addresses of schools previously attended.

For veterans serving after January 1, 1977, the contributory plan consists of a monthly deduction from military salary of $25 to $100 per month, up to a total of $2700, which is deposited in a special training fund. A lump-sum contribution may be made to the fund by participants on active duty. When the benefits are used, the government matches the individual's contribution at the rate of $2 for every $1. Participants draw benefits equal to the number of months they contributed, or 36 months, whichever is less. One can withdraw from the program at the end of any 12-consecutive-month period and still have contributions refunded.

Eligible educational institutions for veterans cover the spectrum and include vocational and business schools, technical institutions, correspondence schools, as well as traditional schools.

Active-duty military personnel generally qualify for military tuition assistance, which will pay up to 75 percent of tuition costs.

Other useful information is that many of the institutions that award credit for military experience use *The Guide to the Evaluation of Educational Experiences in the Armed Services*, published by the American Council on Education, as the basis for their evaluation.

The Defense Activity for Non-Traditional Education (DANTES) "provides official transcripts of scores earned by military personnel," on DANTES Subject Standardized Tests. They do not, as some believe, actually award the credit. The awarding of credit is determined by the individual college or university to which the scores are forwarded.

Education centers, such as the one at the Pentagon, provide testing for active-duty military, and some for Department of Defense civilians. These include the College Level Examination Program (CLEP), the Scholastic Aptitude Test, the American College Test and the Graduate Record Examination. Vocational testing is also available. Such tests as the Strong Campbell Interest Inventory (SCII), the Career Assessment Inventory (CAI), and the Self Directed Search (SDS) are available at some military education centers.

This is the essence of what you need to know. Further information will be available at your base or post education office, or at your local Veterans Administration office.

4
TESTING AND FINANCIAL AID

There has been controversy in recent years about educational testing and the degree to which its results can predict academic performance and success. A corollary to this debate has been the question of whether or not a student can prepare for standardized testing and thereby raise his scores. The testing industry has become a wealthy benefactor of our degree-conscious society, with organizations such as the Educational Testing Service having a major influence over the course of American education.

By the time we are in high school most of us have become accustomed to testing, although very few must like the tremendous impact that it has upon the course of our lives. Almost anyone can be admitted to college today, but admission to the proper preparatory schools, which leads to admission to the proper colleges and to an upwardly mobile career, is dependent upon clearing hurdles, such as academic testing, early in life.

John Holt, the well-known critic of contemporary educational practice, has called the "test-examination-marks business a gigantic racket, the purpose of which is to enable students, teachers, and schools to take part in a joint pretense that the students know everything they are supposed to know."*

Regardless of how the nontraditional student feels about tests, he or she must be able to take them to establish college credits through programs such as CLEP. Moreover, since the student will not be involved in a classroom situation or on a face-to-face basis with his or her mentor/tutor/professor, the ability to take tests and write well become commensurately more important.

Can students "cram" for a standardized test and increase their scores? Most testing specialists and educators claim that this cannot be done, since these tests are based upon cumulative knowledge gained over a lengthy period of time. Yet who can deny the positive effects of practicing mathematics and English grammar in preparation for such standardized tests? This is particularly the case when the student has not been exposed to such subjects recently, or when the student seeks to establish Credit by Examination or through Challenge Examinations.

The corollary question is whether professional organizations that help students prepare for tests are worth the time and money? Is the student better off working alone and investing about $10.00 in one of the many excellent testing practice guides on the market? This is a difficult question whose answer will depend largely upon the abilities of the individual student. One cannot deny, however, that the instructors in these testing centers are very familiar with the various tests, such as the LSAT or MCAT, and have detailed knowledge of what you can expect.

Thus you *can* learn how to take standardized tests and you can increase your scores by the appropriate and diligent preparation for such tests. Educators may claim that the contrary is true, yet what is measured by standardized testing is frequently not one's knowledge base or intelligence but rather one's canniness at ferreting out the correct answer from among four to six choices. Too many traditional educators must defend testing, for otherwise they cannot defend the institution of education as it exists today, a

*John Holt, *What Do I Do on Monday?* (New York: E.P. Dutton, 1970), p. 135.

pedagogic creed that can often stifle curiosity and learning. The prospects for successfully challenging this system on one's own are why lifelong and nontraditional learning are so exciting.

Financial Aid

We are all familiar with the high cost of a college education. There has been a great deal of media coverage about cutbacks by the Reagan Administration in funds for education, as well as cuts in student-loan programs. In fact, there may be a widespread belief that there are no funds available for those who need assistance to pay for college. The fact remains that there are a variety of scholarship and tuition-assistance loan programs still available to the student. In some instances these funds are available to the adult who is returning to school to further or complete his or her education.

While the following list is by no means comprehensive, it is a beginning point for those who are seeking educational funds. The student must bear in mind that it is not necessary to be poor to qualify for financial assistance.

Further information about these programs will be available at the financial office of the school you are attending or considering. Obviously, one can never be certain what will happen to any given Federal program in these times of cutbacks.

Finally, there are many state programs and private scholarship funds available. (This information will also be available in your school's financial aid office.)

FEDERAL STUDENT AID PROGRAMS
PELL GRANT (BASIC EDUCATIONAL OPPORTUNITY GRANT)
The Pell Grant program, which was called the Basic Educational Opportunity Grant, distributes monies directly to students whose eligibility is determined by a Family Contributions Schedule.

Eligible students must prove U.S. citizenship or permanent residence, half-time to full-time attendance at an approved school, family income below the middle to upper-middle level, and enrollment in a program that will take at least nine months.

The Pell Grant program authorizes up to $1670 during 1981–82, an amount that may go up to $1800 in 1982–83. These grants cannot exceed fifty percent of the cost of tuition, after the family contribution has been factored in. Funds from this program are not available to those who already have a bachelor's degree.

You may also receive the Pell Grant even if you are a part-time student.

SUPPLEMENTAL EDUCATIONAL OPPORTUNITY GRANTS
This is a school-administered government program that is dependent upon available funds. Grants range from $200 to $2000; the final amount awarded is dependent upon the school you are attending and the total need of their student body. These funds are

available only to a limited number of students who demonstrate exceptional financial need. These funds need not be repaid.

Eligibility requires U.S. citizenship or permanent residence, half- to full-time attendance.

LAW ENFORCEMENT EDUCATIONAL PROGRAM
This program is for full-time employees of publicly funded state or local law enforcement agencies who are going to school at least half- or full-time. Up to $400 is an outright grant. There is no repayment for amounts above this amount since twenty-five percent of the loan is canceled for each year the individual remains in law enforcement.

COLLEGE WORK-STUDY PROGRAM
Half- and full-time students are eligible, generally based upon proven financial need. About $1500 is available per student per year.

NATIONAL DIRECT STUDENT LOAN
Half- and full-time students are eligible for this program, based on financial need. Fifteen hundred dollars per year is the general maximum, with a cumulative total of $6000. Up to 10 years is allowed to repay this money, and the interest rate charged is low.

SOCIAL SECURITY EDUCATIONAL BENEFITS
Social Security provides funds to the children of deceased, disabled, or retired workers while their children are full-time students between 18 and 22 years of age. The amount awarded will depend on the income the worker was earning when he or she became disabled, retired, or died, but average around $100 monthly.

VETERANS ADMINISTRATION
This information has already been covered in Chapter 3.

5

ABOUT
THIS BOOK

It has been the goal of the compiler of this catalog to make it as accessible and easy to understand as possible. This accounts for the narrative approach, and the absence of an individual listing for each and every course and major offered by each institution. If you are interested in a school's approach a follow-up inquiry to the mailing address provided will quickly secure this type of information for you.

Each institution has different rules and procedures and some are naturally more adept at working with adult learners. If you have any questions that are not answered by this guide, don't hesitate to ask an admissions official at the school you are interested in for an answer. Before enrolling in any program, you should compare several different programs with your particular, and anticipated, needs and requirements.

There will be some who cannot continue their education because of financial considerations. Although this issue has not been thoroughly explored herein, my simple advice to you is that you can find tuition money if you seek it hard enough. Your employer may be willing to pay for part or all of your education. You will also discover that there is more scholarship money around than is commonly known. Each year a substantial number of scholarships go unclaimed. Regardless of your circumstances, a variety of programs has been presented in THE COMPLETE GUIDE TO NONTRADITIONAL EDUCATION, among which are some low-cost alternatives.

The reader will note that some of these listings are slightly longer than others and that different categories of information about programs have been included. None of these variations in length is intended to imply endorsement of any particular program. Each institution solicited has provided information in varying degrees of depth, and this is what accounts for these variations.

All of the programs listed are suited to the mature, self-motivated learner. If for any reason you do not locate precisely the program you seek in this directory, then try contacting your state-university system to check on their programs. Each state-university system has established programs to serve adult learners with continuing education and certification programs, to serve members of the military and business communities, to provide health-training programs, and so forth.

Because of space limitations it has been impossible to include an evaluation of all adult, nontraditional, or continuing-education programs in this catalog. It is the hope of the compiler of THE COMPLETE GUIDE that if this first edition is a success, subsequent editions will keep this publication up-to-date, easy to utilize, and much more comprehensive.

6

STATE LISTS
OF
NONTRADITIONAL
SCHOOLS

Note: The states included appear in alphabetical order and, within each state, individual schools are alphabetized by location. Not every state is listed, but an attempt will be made to do so in future editions.

Alabama

American Institute of Psychotherapy
500 Lowell Drive
Huntsville, Alabama 35801

(205) 536-9088

Background: Founded in 1978 and licensed in January 1980 by the Alabama Board of Education to grant the Doctor of Psychology degree. The American Institute of Psychotherapy (AIP) is not accredited by the Southern Association of Schools and Colleges. This institution's "primary educational objective is the training of students in all aspects of clinical functioning. As a professional school, our primary concern is the training of psychological practitioners. To assure that students are being trained, a milieu must be provided where theory, training, research and practice can all be accommodated."

Admission: Minimum of a bachelor's degree, and a "careful screening" to make certain prospective students are qualified.

Degree Awarded: Doctor of Psychology, Psy. D. This is a professional degree and "more adequately reflects professional training in psychology than the Ph.D., which is, traditionally, an academic research degree."

Tuition: $100 per credit hour.

Study Program: The student must complete 108 trimester hours, a one-year internship, and the Clinical Evaluation Conference. Academic courses at the AIP are only a portion of the program. "An essential aspect of professional education and development is supervised practice in clinical skills." The student must also participate as a client with an "approved therapist" for at least twelve one-hour sessions.

Credit for Life Experience: No.

Time Required: Four years.

New College
External Degree Program
P.O. Drawer ED
University, Alabama 35486

(205) 348-4600

Background: Established in 1970, the New College added the external degree program in 1973.

Admission: Applicant must be over 22 years of age and have a high school diploma or GED equivalency score of at least 50.

Degrees Offered: This interdisciplinary program grants a B.A. or B.S. No graduate credit is available. Typical areas of concentration are: Human Services, Humanities, Social Sciences, Natural Sciences, Applied Sciences, Administrative Sciences, and Communication.

Tuition: $41 per semester hour. There is also an evaluation fee of $50 to $100, depending upon the number of semester hours involved. There is also a standardized evaluation fee of $25 per transaction.

Study Program: 128 semester hours are required for graduation. These credits are broken down as follows: Humanities, 12 semester hours; Social Sciences, 6 semester hours; Natural Sciences, 6 semester hours, Depth Study, 32 semester hours; Electives, 32 semester hours; Final Project, 12 semester hours. The final Project is a "major piece of work—a consolidating experience."

Credit for Life Experience: Yes.

Time Required: "You may work as quickly as your schedule permits, as this is an individualized program." You must complete 128 hours for graduation. "Thirty-two hours of the total hours required, including eight hours of the Depth Study, must be completed under the auspices of the University of Alabama following admission to the New College. This could include course attendance, prior-learning evaluation, Weekend College, television and correspondence courses, and out-of-class contract learning. 'Residence' must be established by the completion of 'work under the auspices' of the University of Alabama . . . ."

Arkansas

Department of Independent Study
University of Arkansas
Fayetteville, Arkansas 72701

(800) 632-0035 (in state only)
(501) 575-3647

Background: State-operated, correspondence study. External high school diploma also available.

Admission: Open. Open-entry, open-exit. Admission to the correspondence program does not constitute admission to the university.

Degrees Awarded: None offered. No more than 30 semester hours of correspondence credit may be applied to a degree at the university.

Tuition: $25 per semester hour for in-state students and $30.00 per semester hour for nonresidents.

Study Program: Routine correspondence study.

Credit for Life Experience: No.

Time Required: About six months per course.

California

Independent Study
University of California Extension
2223 Fulton Street
Berkeley, California 94720

(415) 642-4124
(213) 825-6169 Los Angeles area
(714) 452-3402 San Diego area

Background: These correspondence courses are offered by the state university system. There is a large number of courses offered via correspondence which can be utilized to supplement an external degree program.

31

Admission: Open-entry, open-exit. Admission to correspondence study does not constitute admission to the University of California.

Degrees Awarded: None.

Tuition: Varies according to the course, $90 to $125 being the common range.

Study Program: Routine correspondence study with a required final examination. The final examination weighs heavily in the final grade received. As many as three courses may be taken at one time. No course may be completed in less than three months. No credit by examination is possible.

Credit for Life Experience: No.

Time Required: One year is allowed to complete a course, with a six-month extension.

Century University
9100 Wilshire Boulevard
Beverly Hills, California 90212

(213) 278-1094

Background: The degrees from Century are not accredited by the regional accrediting organization, but they are well and widely accepted in the business sector. Century University is authorized to grant degrees by the California State Office of Private Post-secondary Education to grant bachelor's, master's, and doctoral degrees.

Admission: Open to qualified working professionals.

Degrees Awarded: Bachelor's, master's, doctorate. You may also earn a bachelor/master or a master/doctorate concurrently. A wide selection of majors is available.

Tuition:

Bachelor Degree Program $1895
Master Degree Program $1995
Doctoral Degree Program $2195

CONCURRENT DEGREE PROGRAM
Bachelor/master $2395
Master/doctoral Program $2695

Study Program: Guided independent study, written papers. Dissertations are required of all doctoral students.

Credit for Life Experience: Yes, through extensive portfolio assessment.

Time Required: A minimum of nine months must be devoted to the program you undertake.

City University Los Angeles
1111 Wilshire Boulevard
Los Angeles, California 90017

(213) 481-0950

Background: Founded in 1974, this institution is not accredited but is authorized by the California State Department of Education to grant degrees. All degrees may be earned without campus contact.

Admission: Open to qualified individuals

Degrees Awarded: A.A.; A.S.; B.S.; B.A.; M.A.; M.S.; Ph.D.

Tuition:
Associate Program $2525
Bachelor's Program $2525
Master's Program $3150
Doctoral Program $3275

Study Program: The catalog describes their external degree as "contract learning." A variety of methods may be utilized from home study to the challenge method of establishing credit. The student must also complete a final thesis or project.

Credit for Life Experience: Yes, a student is allowed to earn one-half of the degree requirements via this method.

Time Required: About one year, perhaps less for highly qualified applicants.

Columbia Pacific University
150 Shoreline
Mill Valley, California 94941

(415) 332-7832

Background: This school is "authorized and empowered by the Superintendent of Public Instruction of the State of California (Office of Private Post-Secondary Education) to confer" degrees. *Translation:* These are legal and legitimate degrees, but they are not accredited. They are quite good in the business world but are not always acceptable in academic environs. Thus, you must, before you start, verify that the degree you seek is acceptable for your purposes.

   One different but interesting part of this program is the requirement to "complete the 'Healthscription' instructional process. This is a workbook of self-assessment and informational process which most students find fascinating and valuable."

   Note: "In some cases the degree requirements can be substantially satisfied by a project the student has already completed at the time of application and fully documents for the University records."

Admission: Essentially, this is an open-admission program.

Degrees Awarded: B.A.; M.A.; Ph.D.

Tuition:

Bachelor's Degree Program	$1935
Combined Bachelor's/Master's	$2485
Master's Degree Program	$1935
Combined Master's/Doctorate	$2585
Doctoral Program	$2075

Study Program: Among other tasks, the student must complete an Independent Study Project. Fully off-campus.

Credit for Life Experience: Yes, they provide "full academic credit for documented prior work, life, and educational achievements."

Time Required: There is a reasonable prospect, depending upon your educational and career background, that you can complete a degree within several months at this proprietary institution.

The Graduate School of Human Behavior
368 42nd Street
Oakland, California 94609

(415) 653-2868

Background: Founded in 1979. Authorized to grant degrees by the State of California. Offers programs in Clinical, Educational and Developmental Psychology.

Admission: Applicant must have a master's degree or its equivalent for admission.

Degrees offered: The Doctor of Philosophy in Clinical Psychology or the Doctor of Philosophy in Developmental/Educational Psychology.

Tuition: $1250 per semester.

Study Program: 38 semester hours, B-average minimum, plus dissertation. Classes are held in late afternoon to accommodate working professionals.

Credit for Life Experience: No.

Time Required: About two years, and contact with the campus is required.

California Western University
700 North Main Street
Santa Ana, California 92701

(714) 547-9625

Background: California Western was founded in 1974 and has had more than 4000 students in their programs. One of the better known nontraditional or alternative-education institutions, California Western is well suited to the mature, mid-career professional. Degrees from this institution have wide recognition and acceptability in business and government, and appear to be drawing increasing recognition in academic circles. No contact with the campus is required, a definite plus for many individuals. California Western was granted accreditation by the National Association of Private, Nontraditional Schools and Colleges on June 12, 1981. One excellent aspect of California Western's program is that a student may *concurrently* earn his B.A./M.A. or M.S. or his Master's/Ph.D. He need not hold a bachelor's degree to be admitted into a concurrent degree program.

35

Admission: Relatively open, based upon educational, military, and work background.

Degrees Awarded: California Western has four separate schools, which award the following degrees:

SCHOOL OF ADMINISTRATION AND MANAGEMENT

Degree	*Area of Specialization*
B.S.	Business Administration
B.S.	Management
M.B.A.	Business Administration
Ph.D.	Business Administration
Ph.D.	Management

SCHOOL OF ENGINEERING

Degree	*Area of Specialization*
B.S.	Engineering
M.S.	Engineering
Ph.D.	Engineering

SCHOOL OF BEHAVIORAL SCIENCE

Degree	*Area of Specialization*
B.S.	Psychology
M.S.	Psychology
Ph.D.	Psychology

SCHOOL OF EDUCATION

Degree	*Area of Specialization*
Ed.D.	Education

(The Ed.D. is a doctor of education)

Credit for Life Experience: Yes. The applicant should provide a thorough educational, occupational, and military portfolio, as well as letters of recommendation and an "independent professional reading bibliography."

Time Required: Open-entry, open-exit, self-paced program: "It is difficult to accurately predetermine the length of each student's study program, since no two are exactly the same." If you have a substantial background this program can probably be completed in about nine months to one year.

Tuition: The following fees applied when this guide was prepared. Obviously, tuition fees may rise for any institution, at any time.

DEGREE PROGRAM	*U.S. RESIDENT*	*NON-U.S. RESIDENT*
Bachelor's	$1975	$2375
Master's	$2075	$2475
Doctoral	$2575	$2975
Concurrent Bachelor's/Master's	$2475	$2875
Concurrent Master's/Doctoral	$2975	$3375

Golden Gate University
536 Mission Street
San Francisco, California 94105

(415) 442-7272

Background: Golden Gate University is a private, nonprofit school founded in 1901. It is accredited by the Western Association of Schools and Colleges. The student body of this school is about 10,000, a figure that includes extensive off-campus programs for business and the military. "Through these programs, students may earn degrees entirely on the bases (military)," without attending classes at San Francisco.

Admissions: For graduate students, a bachelor's degree from an accredited institution, minimum of a 2.5 grade-point average, and the Graduate Record Examination or the Graduate Management Admission Test.

Tuition: A fee of $85 per hour for undergraduate courses; $129 per credit hour for graduate courses; $156 per credit hour for Graduate Taxation courses; $175 per credit hour for Doctoral Seminars.

Degrees Awarded: Bachelor's, master's, and Ph.D. programs with an emphasis on business administration and career-oriented programs.

Study Program: Classes are held both on campus and at a number of civilian and military sites throughout the world. There is no correspondence or independent study as such that would enable the student to earn a degree without classes.

Credit for Life Experience: No.

Time Required: At least one year.

New College of California
777 Valencia Street
San Francisco, California 94110

(415) 626-1694

Background: Founded in 1971 as a nontraditional school for the humanities. A public-interest law school was founded in 1973. This school utilizes "open learning methods— small interdisciplinary classes, close association between faculty and students, and independent study." Their Weekend College program is a two-semester completion course combining "independent study, weekend sessions on campus, and credit for prior experiential learning." Varying degrees of contact with the campus is required.

Degrees Awarded: B.A. and M.A. in Poetics, M.A. in Psychology, other programs are available.

Admissions: Relatively wide open. Their catalog states: "Although it is important for the College to know of past successes or failures, it is more important that decisions be based on what is happening with the particular student at the time of application." "SAT or ACT scores are useful but not required." A $25 nonrefundable fee is required for U.S. students.

Credit for Life Experience: Yes. A $300 fee applies to full- and part-time students for the assessment of prior learning experiences. The New College also participates in the CLEP testing program. The final 30 credit hours of a degree must be earned at New College.

Study Program: In the independent-study mode the student has a faculty mentor–advisor. There are three basic methods: an individually designed and self-paced program; study relationships with teachers outside of New College; or, the student may take classes, etc., at other schools.

Tuition: $1500 per semester for full-time students, taking 12 or more semester hours. Part-time students pay $100 per unit.

Time Required: At least two semesters.

Dominican College
1520 Grand Avenue
San Rafael, California 94901

(415) 457-4440, ext. 204

Background: Catholic liberal-arts college for women (now coeducational) founded in 1890. Only 675 students for those who seek a personalized approach. Campus contact is required. Dominican College has an exchange program with several other Catholic colleges around the United States. This college is about one-half hour from the San Francisco area.

Admission: High school diploma with a 2.5 GPA or better. Scholastic Aptitude Tests are not required of those who have been out of high school for more than six years. A minimum of 30 credit hours must be taken at Dominican to earn their diploma.

Degrees Awarded: Bachelor's and master's degrees are offered in a wide variety of programs.

Study Program: Routine classroom work but the small size of the student body (675) and large faculty (100 full- and part-time), makes this a desirable learning environment for the adult student returning for further education and/or self-fulfillment. Independent Study is available for undergraduate students with the agreement of the instructor and Dean of the College.

Tuition: $4450 annually. Scholarship funds may be available.

Credit for Life Experience: Yes, up to 24 credit hours total through any or all of the following methods: first, the Admissions Office staff will review your transcripts; Second, "consider taking the examinations of some courses if you think you are sufficiently prepared," to a maximum of 12 credits. Also one may establish up to 15 credits through CLEP exams; finally, "prepare a portfolio demonstrating your knowledge or experience," which is good for up to 12 credits.

Time Required: At least one year; two semesters and a summer.

Colorado

Center for Lifelong Learning
Division of Continuing Education
University of Colorado at Boulder
Campus Box #178
Boulder, Colorado 80309

(303) 492-8756

Background: This consortium is composed of the five institutions of higher education in Colorado. Certificate and noncredit courses for certificate programs are available.

Admission: Open. The student is not required to submit transcripts or take entrance exams, if they do not wish to earn credit toward a degree. "Enrollment in indepen-

39

dent study courses does not constitute admission to any of the five institutions." You may enroll at any time.

Courses Available: A wide variety of courses are available varying from Anthropology to Political Science and Real Estate. Paralegal Education is now available for career-oriented individuals. This course is equal to 45 hours of classroom time and carries 4.5 Continuing Education Units.

Degrees Awarded: None available through the Colorado Consortium but the "majority of their courses are available for credit toward the Regents External Degree (New York)." Other institutions offering external degrees, for which Colorado credits may be utilized, are:

Regents External Degrees
Cultural Education Center
Albany, New York 12230

External Degree Programs
School of Continuing Studies
Administration Office Building, Room 109
1201 East 38th Street
Indianapolis, Indiana 46205

Individual Studies
University of Northern Iowa
Baker Hall 59
Cedar Falls, Iowa 50613

External Studies
The University of Iowa
W400 East Hall
Iowa City, Iowa 52242

External Student Program
Ohio University
302 Tupper Hall
Athens, Ohio 45701

Naropa Institute
Dept. K
1111 Pearl Street
Boulder, Colorado 80302

(303) 444-0202

Background: "If the Naropa Institute is not unique, it comes closer to being so than any institute within (our) knowledge. . . . Perhaps Naropa's most precious asset is its student body. Each of the team members . . . was impressed. The chairman thought his group . . . the most exciting group of students he had ever met." This quote comes from the Report of the Evaluation Team of the North Central Association of Colleges and Schools, which the Naropa Institute is accredited by. This institution is operated by one of the Buddhist sects offering an education which seeks to develop one's intuition, as well as his or her rational intellect. Founded in 1974. Independent study at the Naropa Institute during one's junior year may be arranged. You must obtain permission in advance of registration from your college/university and from the Institute.

Admission: Open-admissions policy for those not seeking degrees or a certificate.

Tuition: $180 per 3-credit course as of spring 1981.

Degrees Awarded: B.A. in Dance, Poetics, Theater, Buddhist Studies and Buddhist and Western Psychology; M.A. in Buddhist Studies and Buddhist and Western Psychology; one-year certificate program in a variety of areas.

Study Program: Contact with the campus is required as there is no external degree or study.

Credit for Life Experience: No.

Time Required: This will vary but one year is a likely minimum.

Adult Learning Program
University of Denver
John Ragan
University Park Campus
Denver, Colorado 80208

(303) 753-2036

University of Denver
Colorado Women's College
Ms. Candy McCartney
Office of Admissions
Denver, Colorado 80220

(303) 394-6818

Background: This program is available to residents of the area who wish to continue their studies in a supportive environment. This is a private institution.

Admission: "No rigid admissions formula exists."

Tuition: $1710 full time per quarter; $143 part-time per credit hour; $110 per credit hour for the Weekend College.

Degrees Awarded: B.A.

Study Program: Classes meet on alternating weekends during autumn, winter, and spring for 3½ hours.

Credit for Life Experience: No, except through CLEP and transfer credits.

Time Required: A minimum of one year.

University Without Walls
Loretto Heights College
3301 South Federal Boulevard
Denver, Colorado 80236

(303) 936-8441

Background: The University Without Walls (UWW) program was begun at this independent coeducational institution in 1971. About 500 adults have earned their degrees in the UWW since 1971. Although contact with the campus is required, Loretto Heights College also has the Students-at-a-Distance program. This requires contact with the college for initial registration and orientation workshop, the final degree review, and if applicable the intensive advanced-standing workshop.

Admission: Flexible standards but the applicant must show a desire to learn, capacity and the need to work independently, and motivation and creativity in setting one's own goals.

Degrees Awarded: B.A.; 128 semester hours are required for graduation.

Tuition: Part-time tuition is $160 per semester hour; $2450 per learning segment (sixteen-week semester) for full-time students. Their literature states: "A large percentage of UWW students apply for and receive financial aid."

Study Program: Information not available.

Credit for Life Experience: Yes. They apparently place no minimum or maximum on the number of experiential credits the student may earn. "All learning proposed for academic credit remains a *proposal* until it has been evaluated at the evaluation session. Last year, there were 17 proposals and the credits gained ranged from seven to 78." Credit is only granted based on "your demonstrated learning." For those who propose seven or more experiential credits it is necessary to attend the UWW Credit for Life Learning Workshop.
   The following fees apply to experiential credits:

> up to 18 credits — No Charge
> 19–36 credits   — $30
> 37–60 credits   — $50
> 61–78 credits   — $70
> 79 + credits   — $100

Time Required: The final thirty semester hours must be earned as an actively enrolled UWW student.

Connecticut

Charter Oak College
Board for State Academic Awards
340 Capitol Avenue
Hartford, Connecticut 06115

(203) 566-7230
(800) 842-2220 (toll free)

Background: Established in 1973, Charter Oak College is the external program of the Board for State Academic Awards. After enrollment and all official transcripts are received an evaluation is made and a Candidate Status Report issued. A Candidate Status Report is issued quarterly advising the student of how close he or she is to a degree.

Degrees Awarded: B.A., B.S., A.A. and A.S.

Study Program: The student has any official transcripts forwarded and then proceeds to earn credits through college courses and credit by examination. College credits are earned by any of the following methods: (1) college courses; (2) university correspondence courses; (3) nationally accredited noncollegiate courses; (4) military-service school courses; (5) noncollegiate courses accredited by the Board for State Academic Awards; (6) individual special-examination program; (7) proficiency examinations.

Admission: Open-entry, open-exit. Must be 16 or older and have a high school diploma.

Tuition: $125 enrollment fee. Students not living in Connecticut must pay an additional $100 processing fee. There are other fees.

Credit for Life Experience: The BSAA awards credit for "learning acquired through life or work experience whenever such learning can be measured and validated by objective testing procedures acceptable to the Faculty."

Time Required: This factor will depend solely upon the student's background and motivation.

Individualized Degree Program
Trinity College
Hartford, Connecticut 06106

(203) 527-3151

Background: Trinity was founded in 1823 and this program begun in 1973. This is not an external degree, although it is self-paced. Campus contact is required, although one need not necessarily attend classes.

Admission: "Highly selective," requiring capability, motivation and maturity. In addition to an application the applicant must submit "an essay, two recommendations, and all prior academic records and test scores."

Degrees Awarded: B.A.; B.S.

Tuition: One-third lower than on-campus tuition. However, the literature provided did not state 1982–83 tuition.

Study Program: Classroom participation is not directly required although contact with campus will be necessary for advisement purposes. The "study units" undertaken by the student are self-paced courses with detailed study guides. Generally, the student must read a number of books and write several assignments.

Credit for Life Experience: No, except for college credit transferred to Trinity. Also, "regardless of the number of credits accepted, the student must complete at Trinity at least three courses in nonmajor areas, an IDP project, and requirements for the major."

Time Required: You may take as long as ten years to complete this self-paced program with college credits and motivation.

South Central Community College
60 Sargent Drive
New Haven, Connecticut 06511

(203) 789-7069

Background: South Central Community College was established in 1968. It offers general education and career programs. Persons over 62 and veterans who served in time of war, and were/are residents of Connecticut are exempt from tuition but do pay lab fees and for their own books. Students can earn up to 48 hours of credit by nontraditional methods at SCCC.

Admission: Open.

Degrees Awarded: Associate of Arts or Associate of Science. Also offers a variety of one-year certificate programs in subjects like Secretarial Science, Data Processing, and Business Administration. This is a low-cost alternative to private business colleges.

Tuition: $150 for a full-time student with resident status; $570 for out-of-state residents; $10.25 per semester hour for residents; $38.00 per hour for out-of-state students.

Study Program: In addition to routine classroom work, Individualized Instruction and Independent Study are available. Individualized Instruction Permission forms are handed in during registration. The slightly different Independent Study form includes "objectives and justification of the project, the nature of the learning outcomes, learning methodology, and the evaluative criteria. . . ." This document is signed by the student, instructor and the Academic Dean within the first two weeks of classes.

Credit for Life Experience: A student may earn up to 48 semester hours of credit by "achieving acceptable performance levels on examinations or by presenting acceptable documentary evidence of competence." They do not charge regular tuition and fees for these credits but a one-time $15.00 evaluation fee.

Time Required to Complete a Degree: This will depend upon previous educational and occupational background, as well as the quality of the student's portfolio. Students with a 2.0 GPA may transfer to a state college; those with a 2.5 are eligible to transfer to the University of Connecticut.

School of Continuing Education
Eastern Connecticut State College
Willimantic, Connecticut 06226

(203) 456-2231

Background: This program is not the same as The State Board for Academic Awards program also listed herein. Founded in 1889, this institution has the distinction of being the second oldest of Connecticut's state colleges (about 2500 students.)

Admission: High school diploma.

Degrees Offered: B.A.; B.S.; A.S. (Eastern Connecticut also offers a Master of Science degree).

Tuition: 1981–82: $890.00 full-time, in-state; $1830 full-time, out-of-state

Study Program: Evening classes and mini-sessions. Also: "An alternative Learning Design: S.W.E.A.T. is a program that provides work experience which allows students to test their interests and ideas in a given area. The program allows a student to work out his/her own learning design. In addition to presenting an opportunity for self-direction and self-reliance, S.W.E.A.T. provides for a reflective and analytical understanding of the self." CLEP.

Credit for Life Experience: Yes, providing that it is "documentable" and equivalent to the campus course. They will grant as many as 60 semester hours, but this is not frequent. More than a few people have received no credit for life experience.

Time Required: 30 semester hours or one year, including 15 hours of work in your major.

Florida

Embry–Riddle Aeronautical University
College of Continuing Education
Star Route Box 540
Bunnell, Florida 32010

(904) 673-3180

Background: Embry–Riddle offers a solid program for those interested in a career in the aviation industry. With headquarters in Florida, this institution offers their program at a number of locations throughout the United States. A program logically of interest to military personnel, it is approved for Veterans Administration benefits. Accredited by the Southern Association of Colleges and Schools. This is a solid nontraditional, external-degree program offering technical skills as compared to "soft" majors such as sociology and English, which is the general case with nontraditional/flexible education.

Degree(s) Awarded: Bachelor of Professional Aeronautics.

Admission: The Professional Aviation Career Education Degree (PACED) Program is "open to those adults who have graduated from an accredited high school or who have achieved high school equivalency through the general education development (GED) test program with an average of 45 or higher, and a minimum of 40 in each of the five subject areas," according to their literature. Incidentally, this publication has endeavored to cull the quintessence of each institution's literature to allow them to "speak for" themselves, to the greatest extent possible.

Requirements: A total of 129 semester hours in: General Education (33–48 credit hours); Aeronautical Technology (18–48 hours); Aviation-oriented courses, 45 hours minimum. The General Education requirement may be fulfilled through CLEP or the DANTES testing program, or from an accredited institution. *The student may not fulfill the General Education component by independent study with Embry–Riddle.*

Credit for Life Experience: Definitely! This should be of major interest to our military readers. Embry–Riddle's literature states: "Depending upon your aviation teaching and experience, you may be awarded 18 to 48 credit hours for Aeronautical Technology, in recognition of your professional accomplishments in aviation upon verification of your civilian or military aviation training and experience."

Study Program: The textbook, audio-cassette tapes, and the study guide are the pillars of this pedagogic method. The student is allotted three months to complete a course, a more-than-ample period of time for those who hope to graduate before rivaling Methuselah. There are examinations to be taken, for which you must arrange an acceptable proctor.

Tuition: $70 per credit hour, $210 per three-credit-hour course. A $25 application fee. These costs may have risen by the time this information is published.

Time Required: There appears to be no minimum time requirement for this program, which means that it could be expeditious for the experienced military individual.

College for Human Services
Suite #207
4141 N. Andrews Avenue
Fort Lauderdale, Florida 33309

(305) 565-3335

Alida Mesrop, Dean
345 Hudson Street
New York, New York 10014

(212) 989-2002

Harold I. Jackson, Dean
477 15th Street
Oakland, California 94612

(415) 451-6203

Background: Founded in 1964 by Audrey C. Cohen, this institution has branch campuses in Fort Lauderdale, Oakland, California, and New York City. Accredited by the New York State Board of Regents. This program offers full-time study in conjunction with full-time employment. The idea behind study in this college is the application of classroom knowledge to the real world. Credit for each semester, which is called a "crystal," is "awarded only upon successful completion and documentation of such 'constructive action.'" This institution has a "tradition of close collaboration with employers.'

Admission: The applicant must be employed full-time in a human-service position or "qualify for enrollment in a federally funded training program."

Tuition: Tuition at the New York campus is $1672 per "crystal" (semester).

Degrees Awarded: Bachelor of Professional Studies—Human Services degree.

Study Program: Eight semesters, each 16 weeks in length, involving 12 hours of classroom work and 21 hours of work-related application to a real-life situation. Each of the eight "transdisciplinary modules" is called a "crystal," "each of which focuses on a particular practice mode which is critical to human service performance."

Credit for Life Experience: Not in the sense used in this book, wherein a block of credits is granted for previous or experiential learning.

Time Required: "At the College for Human Services, it is possible to earn a bachelor's degree in less than three years while continuing to advance on the job."

Ft. Lauderdale College
1401 East Broward Boulevard
Ft. Lauderdale, Florida 33301

(305) 462-3761

Background: Founded in 1940 as the Walsh School of Business Science. This institution is a member of the Summit System of Colleges and Schools. Ft. Lauderdale is a nonprofit, nonsectarian, coeducational institution. Two bachelor degrees may be earned simultaneously. This is essentially a business college, offering a variety of degrees in accounting, hotel and restaurant administration. Contact with the campus is required.

Admission: High school diploma or equivalent.

Tuition: $45 per credit hour, each course consists of 4.5 credit hours and a full-time student takes 3 classes at a time.

Degrees Awarded: A.S.; B.A.; B.S.

Study Program: Routine study, the nontraditional component being the establishment of credit for learning outside the classroom.

Credit for Life Experience: Yes, through the College Level Examination Program, credit for noncollegiate training and challenge examinations.

Time Required: This will depend solely upon the student but a minimum of one year is likely.

Heed University
Home Federal Tower, 7th Floor
1720 Harrison Street, Young Circle
Hollywood, Florida 33020

(305) 925-1600

Heed University
Suite #310
3923 West 6th Street
Los Angeles, California 90020

(213) 855-0962

Background: Founded in 1970 as a "private, not-for-profit, nonsectarian" institution, Heed is licensed by the State of Florida but is not accredited by the regional accrediting association. Degrees from Heed are accepted in the business world, but they are not accepted for teacher certification, nor are they acceptable prerequisites for examinations administered by the Florida Department of Professional and Occupational Regulation. Heed is seeking "candidate status" for accreditation from the Southern Association of Colleges and Schools. Incidentally, simply because a school is not accredited by one organization, it does not follow that they will not be accredited by others. Heed's program in psychoanalysis is accredited by the National Accreditation Association for Psychoanalysis. Heed offers programs designed for working, professionally oriented adults. Heed University is organized around the concept of a community of scholars.

Admission: Bachelor's degree for admission to a Master's program; a Master's degree is required for admission to a Doctoral program. In addition to an application the student must also submit official transcripts, three letters of recommendation and a professional resume or portfolio.

Degrees Awarded: M.A.; M.B.A; Ed.D.; Ph.D.

Tuition: One hundred dollars per credit hour. There are a number of other fees, such as the Dissertation or Project Continuation Fee of $250. A minimum of about $400 for a Master's, and more for a doctoral program.

Study Program: Heed offers a modified external-degree program that requires some campus contact. Students are "in residence" at a Heed University Center for six or more concentrated one-week interdisciplinary seminars. The scheduling of these seminars is flexible. The other aspect of this program is individualized and supervised independent study. In conjunction with the faculty, the student develops a study plan to be carried out off-campus. Their sample Doctoral Degree Program is as follows:

Initial Assessment and Evaluation . . . up to 6 credits
Post-Master's credit transferable . . . up to 12 credits
On-Campus Seminars, Supervised Independent Studies and
   Research . . . 24 credits
Off-campus Supervised Independent Studies and Research . . . 18–33 credits
Prospectus and Detailed Outline . . . 10 credits
Research Project or Dissertation
(Requires Oral Presentation and Defense) . . . 10 credits

Credit for Life Experience: Yes, through portfolio assessment.

Time Required: About one year; longer for doctoral programs.

State University System
External Degree Program
Florida International University
Miami, Florida 33199

(305) 552-2376

Background: This external-degree program is open exclusively to Florida residents with two or more years of college. It was founded in 1972 and is administered by Florida International University.

Degrees Awarded: Degrees are offered in the School of Technology, School of Education, School of Public Affairs and Services, School of Hospitality Management, School of Business and Organizational Sciences and the College of Arts and Sciences.

52   **Credit for Life Experience:** Yes, the student must develop and submit a portfolio.

Study Program: "The External Degree Program encourages the student to complete approximately 25 quarter hours of supervised learning projects." The student may also take formal classes from any accredited upper-division institution in Florida.

Walden University
801 Anchor Rode Drive
Naples, Florida 33940
(main office)

(813) 261-7277

Walden University
Suite #814
591 Camino de la Reina
San Diego, California 92108

(714) 297-6971

Background: Founded 1970 as a nontraditional university without walls. Walden is not accredited but is licensed to operate in a number of states. Although not accredited, Walden offers a substantial, self-paced, doctoral program. About 1100 people have earned degrees from Walden since its inception. Drawing upon an individual's life experience is a part of the program. In the fall of 1982, Walden announced a doctoral program in which all residency requirements are satisfied by attending one weekend per month for two terms in the Washington, D.C., area.

Degrees Awarded: Ph.D. or the Ed.D.

Admission: A master's degree or at least 30 hours of graduate-level courses, and a minimum of three years' professional experience. The application fee is $45, which is nonrefundable. You will need two letters of recommendation. And official transcripts sent directly from each institution previously attended. If you do not have 30 graduate hours, you may take independent study with Walden, or at an acceptable institution of your choice.

Study Program: Upon acceptance, the student may elect to begin study with the Guided Independent Study Program. This consists of "self-instructional modules which deal with basic preparation for the successful completion of the doctoral program." The second phase is the Residency program, which is four weeks in length. Residency programs have been held in Delaware, Maine, Rhode Island, and California. Dur-

53

ing this phase the student "focuses on the doctoral dissertation he or she is about to undertake, plus a program of core courses." This session culminates in the preparation of the dissertation proposal (which is not as difficult as at first it may appear). Phase Three occurs at home under the long-distance guidance of a personal research advisor, a reader, and "typically members of a recognized graduate faculty." Thus, your faculty may be drawn from a number of different institutions.

Credit for Life Experience: Yes. Experiential Learning Petitions, or your intent to file one, must be submitted prior to the four-week summer-residency session. Fees for evaluation are as follows: 1 to 6 semester hours, $175; 7 to 15 semester hours, $275; 16 or more semester hours $345.

Tuition:

Summer Residency Session	$2195
First Research Term	$2195
Second Research Term	$2195
Third Research Term	$2195

Orlando College
5500–5800 Diplomat Circle
Orlando, Florida 32810

(305) 628-6870

Background: Founded in 1918 and formerly known as Jones College, Orlando College, so named in 1982, is now a member of the Summit System of Colleges and Schools. Accredited by the Association of Independent Colleges and Schools, Orlando is nonprofit, nonsectarian and coeducational. The outlook of this institution is quintessentially nontraditional. The programs offered by this college are all business related, i.e., accounting and real estate.

Admission: High school diploma or equivalent.

Degrees Awarded: B.S.; A.S.

Tuition: $40 per quarter hour.

Study Program: Routine class work, the nontraditional component here being credit for life experience, CLEP, etc.

Credit for Life Experience: Yes. Also, credit may be established through CLEP and proficiency examinations offered by the College, up to 22.5 quarter hours.

Time Required: At least one year.

Eckerd College
5401 — 34th Street South
P.O. Box #12560
St. Petersburg, Florida 33733

(813) 867-1166

Background: Founded in 1958 as Florida Presbyterian College, Eckerd is a liberal arts college. Accredited by the Southern Association of Colleges and Secondary Schools. The Program for Experienced Learners has about 450 students and only accepts persons 25 or older. It is an open-entry program. A student must take nine courses at Eckerd, out of the 36 required for a bachelor's degree. As you read Eckerd's literature and compare it to that of many other institutions, there is a feeling that they understand the adult learner returning to school and are eager to help. Each student has a faculty mentor to assist and guide them through their educational growing process. There is an interdisciplinary approach to many of their majors.

Degrees Granted: B.A.; B.S. Certain majors are related to professional and paraprofessional careers. For example, special majors are available in Criminal Justice and Public Safety Administration.

Admission: Persons 25 or over for the Program for Experienced Learners.

Credit for Life Experience: Yes, the Program for Experienced Learners may accept transfer or life-experience credit for 27 of the 36 courses required for a degree. The student earns such credit by examination or through portfolio preparation.

Study Program: The students may, if they wish, take regular courses at Eckerd. Directed Study Courses do not require class participation and this appears to be a more common route among the individuals participating in Eckerd's Program for Experienced Learners (PEL). The PEL consists of five steps: (1) Admission; (2) Preliminary Assessment of Academic Learning; (3) Directed Study Course, "Life, Learning and Vocation"; (4) Portfolio Assessment and Assessment of Prior Learning Growing out of "Life, Learning, and Vocation"; (5) Preparation of Degree-Completion Plan.

Tuition: A $20 application fee; $150 Portfolio Assessment for Validation of Prior Learning ($35 extra for each course validated); Development of Degree Plan, $70; Directed or Independent Study is $190 per course; $190 per Comprehensive Examination; $297 for each Intensive or Tutorial Course; $190 for the one-credit Thesis Project.

Time Required: To maintain active status in this program, the student must complete three courses per year. Courses are designed to be completed within a four-month period, although extensions will be granted.

University of Sarasota
2080 Ringling Boulevard
Sarasota , Florida 33577

(813) 955-4228

Background: Nontraditional program of "supervised individual research and writing combined with intensified research and writing combined with intensified residence activities that yield a maximum of student-faculty interaction." Although the University of Sarasota is licensed to grant degrees, they may not automatically qualify you for professional examinations or licensure in Florida, or elsewhere. The University of Sarasota is a candidate for accreditation with the National Association of Private, Nontraditional Schools and Colleges located in Colorado. Contact with the campus is required.

Admission: 60 semester hours with a minimum of 2.0 for admission to the Baccalaureate program. A bachelor's degree from an accredited institution and 18 semester hours of work in business or a related field for admission into the MBA program.

Degrees Offered: A.B.; M.A.; Ed.D. They have a School of Management and Business and a School of Education.

Tuition: Ninety-five dollars per semester hour; $400 for three-semester credit tutorials; $500 for the Directed Problem Study consisting of four semester hours. There are a variety of fees for credit assessment, $450 commencement and support service fees, etc.

Study Program: "Programs consist of a combination of classes, seminars, supervised individual work and appropriate testing."

Credit for Life Experience: Yes, the School of Management and Business offers the "possibility of receiving course credit for life experiences, professional expertise and nondegree training." Advanced standing is possible this way.

Time Required: At least two semesters is likely.

Bachelor of Independent Studies
External Program
University of South Florida
Tampa, Florida 33620

(813) 974-4058

Background: The University is part of the State University System, and was founded in 1960. "The principal difference between the BIS (Bachelor of Independent Studies) Degree and other baccalaureate degrees is the absence of a disciplinary major and the uniqueness of the combined methods of study." This program is geared to the needs of adult learners. The Bachelor of Independent Studies program was instituted in 1969.

Admission: High school diploma or GED.

Degrees Offered: B.A.

Tuition: Total cost of tuition and fees is $3750, payable as you progress through the program.

Study Program: Guided independent study, residential seminars, and a thesis. A degree of contact with campus is required. The student must be in touch with his advisor at least once a month. Each area or subject seminar involves three weeks on campus and is offered in June, July, or August.

Credit for Life Experience: Yes, there are "two-waiver and an abbreviated reading program" methods of receiving credit.

Time Required: At least one year.

Georgia

Independent Study
Georgia Center for Continuing Education
The University of Georgia
Athens, Georgia 30602

(404) 542-3243

Background: All courses offered are on the undergraduate level. The Independent Study program is open to anyone, and transcripts of prior work are not required.

Degrees Awarded: Not available.

Study Program: Not available.

Credit for Life Experience: No.

Tuition:
   3 quarter-hour course, $72.
   4 quarter-hour course, $96.
   5 quarter-hour course, $120.

Illinois

University Without Walls
Chicago State University
9500 South King Drive
Chicago, Illinois 60628

(312) 995-2455

Background: Chicago State offers the Illinois Board of Governors degree and has the University Without Walls program requiring low campus contact. This program is for people over the age of 23.

Admission: Previous college experience is desirable but not required.

Tuition: The same as any full-time Chicago State student.

Degrees Awarded: B.A.; the Board of Governors degree lists "Independent Studies" as your major.

Study Program: A learning agreement proposal is submitted at the beginning of the term which "lists a logical sequence of educational activities and objectives." The 120 hours required for graduation may be earned in a number of ways.

Credit for Life Experience: Yes, and credit may be established through CLEP, and the Proficiency Examination Program.

Time Required: Their literature is unclear regarding the UWW program. However, you must take 15 credit hours of classroom work at Chicago State to earn the Board of Governors degree.

DePaul University
School for New Learning
23 East Jackson Boulevard
Chicago, Illinois 60604

(312) 321-7901

Background: This program was established in 1972 to serve adults over 24 years of age. The School for New Learning is interested in competencies instead of official college credits. Competence is demonstrated in five areas: (1) The World of Work; (2) Communication and Interpersonal Relations; (3) The Human Community; (4) Quality of Life; (5) Lifelong Learning. This program will only work for those in the Chicago area since contact with the campus is required.

Admission: All students begin by taking the Discovery Workshop, a three-day self assessment seminar which costs $198.00. New students are admitted each month.

Degree Awarded: Bachelor of Arts.

Study Program: The idea behind this program is to teach problem-solving skills that can be used in daily life. Once the student establishes ability in the five areas of competence, which is self-paced, he or she can graduate.

Credit for Life Experience: Yes.

Tuition: $73 per quarter hour. "The cost of an individual's program depends upon the number of life experience credits that can be awarded as well as on the individual's educational goal." The minimum cost of a B.A. degree at the School for New Learning is $3659.

Time Required: The school estimates from one to five years.

Correspondence Study Division
Loyola University of Chicago
820 North Michigan Avenue
Chicago, Illinois 60611

(312) 670-3018

Background: Founded in 1870 as St. Ignatius College and operated by the Society of Jesus (i.e., the Jesuits), this is an urban-environment campus. There is a wide selection of courses, from Accounting to Theology.

Admission: Open-entry, open-exit. Admission to correspondence study does not constitute admission to the university.

Degrees Awarded: None through external/correspondence study.

Tuition: A fee of $110 per semester hour.

Study Program: No more than two courses may be taken at one time. A final examination is required, and it counts for 75 percent of the grade.

Credit for Life Experience: No.

Time Required: Maximum of one year, minimum of 12 weeks. A six-month extension can be requested.

Mundelein College
Director of Adult Degree Programs
202 Skyscraper
6363 North Sheridan Road
Chicago, Illinois 60660

(312) 262-8100, ext. 405

Background: An urban Catholic college founded in 1929 by the Sisters of Charity of the Blessed Virgin Mary. Their Continuing Education program was founded in 1965 and was the first of its type in the Midwest. Contact with the campus is required. Independent study is available, but only 12 semester hours may be applied toward graduation. Under their Contractual College Degree program, the student creates his or her own degree, based upon the fulfillment of several criteria. "In this program, students may be able to complete a degree without accumulating 120 credit hours per se, if they can demonstrate competence in the objectives they and the college have spelled out in the contract."

Admission: High school diploma, or equivalent. While the admissions process is not open, and is selective, Mundelein appears to understand the needs and problems of adult learners.

Tuition: $384 per course; $134.40 per 3-semester-hour course awarded for experiential learning.

Degrees Awarded: B.A.; B.S.; Bachelor of Fine Arts.

Study Program: The Contractual College Degree program allows a high degree of flexibility. Other modes of study are flexible but more or less traditional.

Credit for Life Experience: Yes, through their Credit for Academically Relevant Experience program. Credits earned through the CARE program *do not* satisfy the residency requirement. Credits may also be transferred to Mundelein and established through CLEP.

Time Required: At least one year.

Lewis University
Route 53
Romeoville, Illinois 60441

(815) 838-0500

Background: Small, private Catholic institution founded in 1949 under the Christian Brothers. The nontraditional component of their program is the Bachelor of Elected Studies. Up to 72 semester hours of credit may be transferred to Lewis from junior or senior colleges.

Admission: High school diploma or GED.

Tuition: An average of 16 credits per semester is $2160.

Degrees Awarded: In addition to their bachelor's and master's programs, Lewis offers a Bachelor of Elected Studies.

Study Program: Once admitted, the student and his or her counselor plan the course of study. For those who elect the Bachelor of Elected Studies, planning a program is part of the admission process. The BES is "appropriate for students whose individual needs are best met through a broad, interdisciplinary education." One hundred and twenty-eight semester hours are required, including 20 semester hours of upper-division coursework, and the completion of "an individually designed concentration of at least 40 credits of coursework."

Credit for Life Experience: Yes, through any or all of the following: "credit for experience, departmental proficiency examinations, the College Level Examination Program (CLEP), or credit for military training."

Time Required: At least one and a half years, and probably a minimum of two.

Board of Governors Degree
544 Iles Park Place
Springfield, Illinois 62718

(217) 782-6392

Background: The Board of Governor's B.A. degree was "expressly designed for the working adult, and the requirements and nature of the degree were developed to make it possible for qualified adults to earn a college degree while pursuing careers involving work and family responsibilities. With this in mind, the two key features of this degree program that set it apart from others are its flexibility and the fact that adults can receive credit towards degree completion by evaluation of their adult learning experiences that are college equivalent. Although this latter aspect often results in acceleration of this undergraduate degree completion, the primary intent of the program is to make college education available to adults in a way that is compatible with their life style and responsibilities, and to recognize that college-equivalent learning and skills can be achieved in a great variety of ways." Only 15 semester credits need actually be taken at any of the Board of Governors universities.

Admission: Requirements for admission vary somewhat from school to school. Governors State University requires at least 60 semester hours for admission, but this may be done through experiential learning.

The local schools operating this program are:

Board of Governors Degree
Chicago State University
95th Street at King Drive
Chicago, Illinois 60628

(312) 995-2213

Board of Governors Degree
Governors State University
Park Forest South, Illinois 60466

(312) 534-5000

Board of Governors Degree
Western Illinois University
Macomb, Illinois 61455

(309) 298-1929

Board of Governors Degree
Eastern Illinois University
Charleston, Illinois 61920

(217) 581-5618

Board of Governors Degree
Northeastern Illinois University
Bryn Mawr at St. Louis Avenue
Chicago, Illinois

(312) 583-4050

Board of Governors Degree
Western Illinois University
for Continuing Education
The John Deere School
910 18th Avenue
East Moline, Illinois 61244

(309) 755-3461

Degrees Awarded: B.A.

Tuition: Off-Campus Tuition Schedule applies to "coursework by mail, radio, television, or newspaper."

Undergraduate Tuition	Illinois Resident	Out of State
Full-Time (12 hours or more)	$513.00	$1539
Part-Time (per hour)	$ 42.75	$ 128.75

Study Program: This is a very flexible program being "highly indivdualized," The student works with a counselor at the location of choice; 120 semester hours are required.

Credit for Life Experience: Yes, for all types of experiences: CLEP tests, United States Armed Forces Institute courses (which is now DANTES), credits from telecourses, correspondence courses from accredited colleges and universities, American College Testing Proficiency Examination.

Time Required: These will vary according to your educational and work background. However, here is a legitimate and accredited program which many individuals should be able to complete in a year or less.

Adult Degree in Liberal Learning Program
Springfield College in Illinois
1500 North Fifth Street
Springfield, Illinois 62702

(217) 525-1420

Background: This program began in the Fall of 1982, and "emphasizes credit for prior learning and life-long learning through a competency-based liberal arts curriculum." The focus is upon "competencies" rather than specific courses, thus upon developing life-long learning skills. Campus contact is required.

Admission: At least 21 years of age, or a high school diploma or equivalent plus dependent children.

Degrees Awarded: Associate of Arts, which "generally is expected" to lead to a B.A. "This degree continues the fine quality of liberal arts preprofessional curricula that has been the mark of Springfield College for over fifty years."

Tuition: A fee of $58 per semester hour.

Study Program: Students first conduct a self-assessment, which is the "basis for planning personal, career and educational goals and will result in individualized degree plans."

Credit for Life Experience: Yes: portfolio development; CLEP; challenge or proficiency examinations.

Time Required: This will depend upon the student and his or her educational and experiential background.

Indiana

Indiana Business College
802 North Meridian Street
Indianapolis, Indiana 46204

(317) 634-8337

Background: This fully accredited institution, established in 1902, has 10 affiliates throughout the state, training approximately 3000 students year-round. They focus on developing competency "rather than completing required hours." IBC operates an employment and placement service, which is "maintained for the benefit of students, former students, and employers without cost."

Admission: A high school diploma. Others may be accepted for special training. IBC is authorized to enroll nonimmigrant students.

Tuition and Terms: Tuition is payable monthly and there are no contracts or registration fees. Effective July 1, 1982, fees are:
$175.00 per month for full-time students
$110.00 per month for half-day students
$50.00 per month for evening school

Programs Offered: Administrative Secretarial Course—14 months, 61 weeks, 1525 classroom hours; Executive Secretarial Course—12 months, 52 weeks, 1300 classroom hours; Private Secretarial Course—9 months, 39 weeks, 975 hours; Professional Accounting Course—24 months, 104 weeks, 2600 classroom hours; Administrative Accounting Course—18 months, 78 weeks, 1950 classroom hours; Accounting Technology Course—14 months, 61 weeks, 1525 classroom hours; Bookkeeping and Machines Course—9 months, 39 weeks, 975 classroom hours; Receptionist and Clerk-Typist Course—6 months, 26 weeks, 650 classroom hours; Stenographic Course—6 months, 26 weeks, 650 classroom hours.

Example of Typical Program:

ADMINISTRATIVE SECRETARIAL COURSE

Course Number	Title	Semester Hours
A101	Single Proprietorship Accounting	4
A102	Partnership Accounting	5
A103	Income Tax Procedures	3
A104	Payroll and Social Security Taxes	1
A105	Corporation Accounting	5

M101	Rapid Calculation	2
M102	Business Mathematics	5
L101	Business Law	4
G101	Management and Human Relations	2
G102	Penmanship	2
E101	Vocabulary and Drill Words	4
E102	Business English	4
E103	Business Letters	1
S101	Shorthand Theory	6
S102	Junior Dictation and Transcription	2
S201	Senior Dictation and Transcription Medical and Legal Dictation	3
S202	Secretarial Procedures Charm Personality Development Office Etiquette	1
T101	Typing—Fundamentals	4
T102	Typing—Practical Applications	4
T201	Typing—Rhythm and Speed Building	4
ADP101	Automation—Input Systems (Keypunch)	1
T202	Machine Transcription	1
G103	Filing	2
S301	Office Practice	1

Iowa

Upper Iowa University
Coordinated Off-Campus Degree Program
Fayette, Iowa 52142

(800) 553-4150 (outside Iowa)
(800) 632-5954 (inside Iowa)

Background: Founded in 1855 under the auspices of the Methodist Church, this institution became independent in 1928. Accredited by the North Central Association of Colleges and Secondary Schools. The Coordinated Off-Campus Degree Program was founded in 1973. Limited campus contact of two to four weeks is required for graduation.

Admission: Must have a high school diploma or equivalent, and no less than a 2.0 GPA.

Degrees Awarded: B.A. with majors in Business Administration or Public Administration.

Requirements: A minimum of 124 semester hours and no less than a 2.0 GPA. In addition to the 30 semester hours of independent study and the residency session, the student seeking a B.A. must also have: six semester hours of Fine Arts; six semester hours of Basic Composition and Introduction to Literature; six semester hours of History; six semester hours of Natural Science.

Study Program: Directed independent study and a residency period of two to four weeks. Each directed independent study module is equal to six credits. Their catalog advises that "frequent contact between students and professors is maintained through telephone consultations," which are toll free. As noted, two weeks' residency is required for those entering with more than sixty credit hours, and four weeks is required for those entering Upper Iowa with less than sixty credits. During campus residency the student completes a four-semester-hour course in his or her major. This residency requirement is at one's convenience. Twelve semester hours is a full off-campus load.

Credit for Life Experience: Yes. Also, up to 30 hours of credit may be established by CLEP, PEP, or DANTES.

Tuition: A $50 application fee; $75 per semester hour; $50 Conversion Fee per module for credit for curriculum-related daily work. $110 per semester hour for On-Campus Residency.

Time Required: The student must complete thirty semester hours by directed independent study, and 4 to 7 hours in residence. No less than one year will be required to graduate from Upper Iowa.

Kansas

Degree Completion Program
Director of Admissions
Benedictine College
Atchison, Kansas 66002

(913) 367-5340
(913) 367-6110

Background: The roots of this institution go back to 1858. It is a Catholic institution offering liberal-arts and science programs. The institution offers a specific degree completion program for military personnel. Military personnel who have served three years or more are awarded eight semester hours as elective credit.

Admission: High school diploma.

Tuition: A fee of $1850 per semester for full-time students; $155 per semester hour for part-time students.

Degrees Awarded: B.A.; B.S.

Study Program: Routine study, no correspondence courses are available.

Credit for Life Experience: Yes, as stated above. Also, through CLEP. Credit will be granted for service schools comparable to courses taught at Benedictine.

Time Required: At least 24 semester hours must be completed at Benedictine, with 12 hours in the major field.

Division of Continuing Education
The University of Kansas
Continuing Education Building
Lawrence, Kansas 66045

(913) 864-4792
(800) 532-6772 (toll free in Kansas)

Background: This is a typical program of correspondence study. It is possible to earn a major portion of a degree at the University of Kansas through independent study: "To obtain a bachelor's degree from the University of Kansas, you are required to earn the last 30 hours of credit in residence. You may petition your dean for a waiver of this rule." There is no graduate credit available through independent study. High school completion courses are also available.

Admission: Open-entry/open-exit; enrollment in independent study does not constitute admission to the University of Kansas.

Tuition: A fee of $30 per semester hour; postage and handling of $15 per course; instructional materials, $15 per course.

Degrees Awarded: None.

Study Program: Examinations are required.

Credit for Life Experience: No.

Time Required: Nine months are allowed to complete a course with one three-month extension. No more than five assignments may be submitted within a seven-day period.

Kentucky

Spalding College
851 South Fourth Street
Louisville, Kentucky 40203

(502) 585-9911

Background: Founded in 1814, Spalding is a four-year fully accredited institution "in the Catholic tradition." Located in downtown Louisville, this college makes every effort to accommodate the mature adult returning for further education. Contact with the campus is required. "Persons 65 or older may enroll, without tuition, in any regular non-laboratory undergraduate or graduate course at Spalding."

Admission: High school diploma or its equivalent.

Degrees Awarded: Bachelor of Arts and the Bachelor of Science and the Master of Arts in a wide variety of fields.

Study Program: For the nontraditional student, classes are held evenings and weekends. Independent Study is also an option when a course of study is not in the regular curriculum. Weekend College students attend classes on five weekends during a normal 12–13 week term.

Credit for Life Experience: To a certain degree, yes. Twelve credit hours of correspondence and extension work may be applied toward a Spalding degree.

Tuition: $1450 per semester for a nonresident commuter for 12—18 credit hours; $3000 for 36 credit hours consisting of two semesters and summer session. A fee of $90 per undergraduate credit hour; $95 per graduate credit hour.

Time Required: A minimum of two semesters appears likely.

Murray State University
Extended Education
Murray, Kentucky 42071

Background: Routine correspondence study. Murray State is part of the University of Kentucky system. Other schools in the system offering correspondence courses are: Eastern Kentucky University, Morehead State University, Western Kentucky University, and the University of Kentucky. Whenever there is a large enough number of students who want a specific course, Murray State will organize a class, if that is practical. High school courses are also available.

Admission: High school diploma.

Degrees Awarded: None available through correspondence study.

Tuition: A fee of $26 per semester hour.

Study Program: Routine correspondence study. No more than 32 semester hours of a baccalaureate may be earned via correspondence. Final examinations are required.

Credit for Life Experience: No.

Time Required: One year is allowed to complete a course, and no three-semester hour course may be finished in less than five weeks. No time extensions are allowed.

Louisiana

Department of Correspondence Study
Division of Continuing Education
Louisiana State University
Baton Rouge, Louisiana 70803

(504) 388-3171
(800) 272-8019

Background: Admission to correspondence study does not constitute admission to Louisiana State University. The 175 correspondence courses offered may be used for a LSU degree and are equivalent to similar courses at other colleges and universities around the country. LSU has a noncredit course for fire-department officer candidates entitled Fire Service Instructor I. High school courses are also offered. LSU students must secure permission from the dean of their college to use correspondence credits toward a diploma. No graduate credit is available. There is a wide selection of courses offered.

Degrees Awarded: No external degrees are awarded.

Admission: Open.

Tuition: A fee of $40 for a 2-hour course; $55 for a 3-hour course; $95 for 4–6 hours; $120 for 7–8 hours; $145 for 9–10 hours.

Study Program: Routine correspondence study. A final examination is required at the end of a course, which must be passed for credit to be awarded. If you live out of state, the test may be taken from a college administrator or under the supervision of a Test Control Officer, if you are engaged in military service.

Time Required: Courses must be completed within nine months.

Southeastern University
5163 General de Gaulle Drive
New Orleans, Louisiana 70114

(504) 392-7157

Background: Contact with the campus is required during the one-month summer residency. Southeastern is a private institution, "appropriately chartered under the laws of Louisiana."

Admission: A master's degree from an accredited school. In some instances professional achievement will be accepted in lieu of a degree.

Degrees offered: Ph.D. in "any field approved by the university's Policy Board."

Tuition: A fee of $995 per semester, with a minimum of three semesters.

Study Program: This will vary according to the program chosen by each student and the types of resources they have available.

Credit for Life Experience: Yes, their brochure states: "All programs operate on the policy of systematic exemption from requirements for which students already have substantial experiential or occupational equivalency."

Time Required: A minimum of three semesters. Their brochure states that most students complete the program in one year.

Maryland

**Office of Continuing Education
Hood College
Frederick, Maryland 21701**

(301) 663-3131, ext. 375

Background: Founded in 1893 by the United Church of Christ as a liberal arts college for women. This is a strong program with the proper understanding of, and orientation toward, the problems of women. Admission to Hood College special programs is without regard to sex, race, or creed. Contact with the campus is required.

Admission: Applicants must be 25 or older for admission to the Hood Experiential Learning Portfolio (HELP). An interview with the Director of Continuing Education is required.

Degrees Offered: B.A.; Bachelor of Science in Home Economics; B.S. in Medical Technology; B.S. in Radiologic Technology.

Tuition: A fee of $165 per credit hour; full-time is 12 semester hours to 17 semester hours and is $5510 per year (1982–83).

Study Program: Continuing-education students have the option of previewing a course for a $25-per-semester-hour fee. At the end of seven weeks (midterm) they are converted to regular-student status unless the student notifies the registrar otherwise. At this point the student pays the balance of the tuition due. "There is a limit of 12 credits of independent work in a student's degree program."

Credit for Life Experience: Yes, through portfolio assessment, challenge examinations, CLEP, military training. Anywhere from one to 30 credits may be awarded for a portfolio.

Time Required: A minimum of one academic year is required.

Massachusetts

Boston University
Overseas Programs
143 Bay State Road
Boston, Massachusetts 02215

(617) 353-3028

Background: The Boston program is one of many operated overseas by the military for the benefit of service personnel. Since this program was founded in 1964, about 3800 students have earned master's degrees. About 1200 are currently enrolled. This program is for graduate students only, but there are other programs operated by the University of Maryland and by other universities for undergraduates as well as for graduate students.

Admission: A bachelor's degree or the equivalent is required. You must also be in the military, or a DOD civilian employee, and have at least two years remaining on your European tour of duty.

Tuition: A fee of $150 per graduate hour. This fee will be raised in early 1983.

Degrees Awarded: M.A. (International Relations); Master of Education (Ed.M.) in Human Services, Counseling, and Special Education; Certificate of Advanced Study in Human Services; Master of Science in Business Administration; Master of Science in Computer Information Systems; M.S. in Nursing.

Study Program: Routine course study through evening and weekend study. A very limited amount of Directed Study is available.

Credit for Life Experience. No.

Time Required: Each of these programs requires at least two years, and some take three.

Elderhostel
100 Boylston Street
Boston, Massachusetts 02116

Elderhostel is a program for adults 60 and older who are interested in "low-cost, short-term residential academic programs." The programs offered by the more than 600 colleges, universities, and other types of educational institutions generally begin on a Sunday evening and end the next Saturday.

There are no exams, grades, or homework for these noncredit courses. "Lack of formal education is not a barrier," since this program is open to all. Class sizes range from 35 to 45.

The cost for 1983 is $180 per course. This is the *total* fee for the classes, room and board, and other extracurricular activities. This is not, however, a sightseeing tour, and those who might want to tour an area should make arrangements to do so before or after the classes.

Elderhostel publishes a tabloid-sized newspaper catalog that can be obtained by writing to the address above. Programs are available not only in the United States but in Canada and Europe as well. There is apparently considerable interest in this type of nontraditional education designed to intellectually stimulate people over 60, since the number of classes and openings available has doubled from 1982 to 1983.

Registration for Elderhostel programs is handled by mail only, and telephone reservation requests are not taken.

Elderhostel programs are designed for anyone over 60. As their catalog says, "Whether you finished grade school or earned a Ph.D., if you have an adventuresome spirit, you're perfect for Elderhostel."

Massachusetts Department of Education
Bureau of Community Education and Adult Services
31 St. James Avenue
Boston, Massachusetts 02116

(617) 727-5784

Background: This organization offers about 60 high school and noncredit courses. Tuition is free to World War II, Korean, and Vietnam War veterans who are residents of Massachusetts. Members of the military currently stationed in Massachusetts, the legally blind, persons over 65, and prisoners in Massachusetts also receive free tuition, as do patients in state, county, and Federal hospitals.

For more detailed information, write to the address above.

Division of Graduate & Continuing Education
Framingham State College
100 State Street
Framingham, Massachusetts 01701

(617) 620-1441

Background: The roots of this school go back to 1839. Although contact with this campus is required, this is a largely external degree program. "A campus contact requirement must be completed by all students prior to being awarded a degree. The requirement is satisfied by completing 24 semester hours of course work or approved sponsored experiences at Framingham State College." 128 semester hours are required for a Bachelor's degree.

Admission: High school diploma or equivalence. There is also a prescreening interview and an admission interview.

Tuition: A fee of $35 per semester hour; $250.00 Procession and Advising Fee.

Degrees Awarded: B.A.; B.S.

Study Program: Their literature states: "Credit may be earned in a number of ways other than by formal course work in order to avoid having to spend a vast amount of time on the college campus." Students do not have a major with this program, conceivably a plus for many.

Credit for Life Experience: Yes.

Time Required: At least one year.

Center for Lifelong Learning
Curry College
Milton, Massachusetts 02186

(617) 333-0500

Background: Founded in 1879, this is an "independent, coeducational, four-year, accredited, professionally oriented liberal arts" college. Contact with the campus is required. Student body of about 1200. The Center also offers several telecourses.

Citizens over 60 years of age may audit two courses per semester without charge, on a space-available basis. You must pay the registration fee.

Admission: High school diploma or equivalent.

Degrees Awarded: A.A.; B.A. and B.S.

Tuition: One to fifteen credits is $65 per hour.

Credit for Life Experience: Yes, via portfolio assessment and through credit by examination.

Time Required: At least two semesters.

Division of Continuing Studies
Southeastern Massachusetts University
North Dartmouth, Massachusetts 02747

(617) 994-9681

Background: This university system offers a variety of methods for earning a significant portion of a degree off-campus. Contract learning, directed study, and independent study. There is no tuition charge for persons 59 or older. Contact with the campus is required for this program.

Admission: Open-entry, open-exit. Admission to correspondence study does not constitute admission to the university.

Degrees Awarded: It is possible to earn a B.A. or B.S. in the following disciplines: English; History; Humanities and Social Sciences; Multi-Disciplinary Studies; Psychology; Political Science; Portuguese; Sociology; Accounting and Management.

Tuition: A fee of $45 per undergraduate credit; $65 per graduate credit.

Study Program: A variety of methods is available.

(1)Contract learning is open to SMU students with over 30 semester hours. Normally the student is a junior or senior. "The project must be a learning experience for the student and must be related to an academic discipline. The experience may be in connection with a job, volunteer work or special project and does not have to be related to a student's major." A maximum of six semester hours may be earned through contract learning.

(2) Directed study is for students who wish to take a course during a semester when it is not being offered. This requires permission from a faculty member, major Department Chairperson, and Dean.

(3) Independent study is available to students with 54 or more semester hours. Up to 12 semester hours may be earned through independent study.

Credit for Life Experience: CLEP and challenge examinatons are available but there is no credit for experiential learning as such.

Time Required: Not available.

Adult Degree Program
Atlantic Union College
So. Lancaster, Massachusetts 01561

(617) 365-4561, ext. 301

Background: The Adult Degree program is open to adults 25 or older. Most of those accepted have a year or more of successful college study or its equivalent. Contact with the campus is required for two-week intensive seminars, in January and July. Atlantic was founded in 1882 by the Seventh-Day Adventist denomination, is co-educational, and "welcomes qualified students who are interested in education structured on Christian principles." This is an excellent "free form" program for the self-directed adult learner who can attend the two required seminars annually.

Admission: At least one year of college work, and applicants must be over 25 years of age.

Degrees Awarded: B.S.; B.A.

Tuition: A fee of $1670 for one unit of study, which is 16 semester hours.

Study Program: During the seminar period the student's work for the next half year is planned. The student is under the supervision of a teacher but is "responsible for organizing large areas of study about which they particularly want to learn." The student has tremendous flexibility to shape his or her education with this program.

Credit for Life Experience: Yes, at a cost of $100 to $150 per unit. A maximum of two units may be earned for experiential learning. A maximum of four units may be earned through CLEP exams.

Time Required: A minimum of two units is required for graduation; one year is the minimum required.

Michigan

Admissions Department
Adrian College
Adrian, Michigan 49221-2575

(517) 265-5161

Background: Founded in 1845, this private, liberal arts college is affiliated with the United Methodist Church. One hundred and twenty-four semester hours are required for graduation.

Admission: Adult students must submit transcripts of high school and any college work. Open-entry for veterans.

Tuition: $4776 full-time tuition.

Degrees Awarded: A.A.; B.A.; B.S.

Study Program: Routine study course.

Credit for Life Experience: Yes, with a limitation of 10 semester hours toward the A.A. and 20 toward the bachelor's degree. CLEP is limited to 15 semester hours. Under the American College Testing, Proficiency Examination Program, a student is limited to 20 semester hours on the A.A., and 40 semester hours on the bachelor's degree. There is a thirty-credit maximum for Servicemen's Opportunity College credits.

Time Required: At least one year and probably longer.

Minnesota

Extension Independent Study
University of Minnesota
Twin Cities
45 Westbrook Hall
77 Pleasant Street, S.E.
Minneapolis, Minnesota 55455

(612) 373-3256

Background: A large number of courses are offered through correspondence, television, radio, newspapers, video cassette, and audio cassette. This program is also connected to the University Without Walls program, through which a degree may be earned. Some credits offered via television may be applied toward a master's degree. The large number of courses available through this program should be of some utility to those completing degrees elsewhere but having difficulty in nailing down all requirements. There are also a number of Extension Certificate Programs, such as Associate in Management of Administrative Services Certificate, Human Services Certificate, Industrial Relations Certificate, and a Junior and Senior Accounting Certificate.

Admission: You may enroll at any time.

Degrees Awarded: A.A.; the Bachelor of Applied Studies and Bachelor of General Studies may not be earned entirely through independent study, although a significant amount of work may be.

Tuition: A fee of $22.50 per credit to $26.50 per credit.

Study Program: A study guide maps out the course, there are lessons to prepare based on required readings. Their catalog states that six to ten hours are required to complete each lesson, including any written assignments.

Credit for Life Experience: No.

Time Required: A recommended minimum of three months to complete a course; there is also a one-year maximum.

University Without Walls
201 Westbrook Hall
77 Pleasant Street, S.E.
Minneapolis, Minnesota 55455

(612) 373-3919
(612) 589-2211

Background: Founded in 1971, efforts are currently under way to expand this program to a number of other locations throughout the state. University Without Walls is a program of the University College, which is one of 22 colleges that constitute the University of Minnesota. University College was founded in 1930 as a "pioneering effort to provide flexibility in degree planning to students whose needs could not be met through existing programs." The student is responsible for developing his or her program. Contact with the campus is not required, but students are encouraged to meet with their advisers, if at all possible. (This program should be of use to the incarcerated, since the school's literature makes specific admission for those in this situation.)

Admission: Applicants must "explain satisfactorily why the UWW program is an appropriate way in which to pursue their studies." Also, applicants must present a "general description of their academic field(s) of study." Advisers in these fields must be available before you will be admitted. Applicants must "identify overall degree objectives that are attainable through University Without Walls." The applicant must also "demonstrate the ability to conceptualize specific learning goals and identify realistic ways to accomplish them." Finally, applicants must have good communication skills.

Degrees Offered: B.S.; B.A.; A.S.

Tuition: A fee of $345 per quarter was the fee in 1980–81. The school's brochure now lists this as "void," without providing a current figure.

Study Program: This program is student designed, grants credit for life or work experiences, utilizes different learning activities, and combines liberal education with individual career goals.

Credit for Life Experience: Yes, after very careful review.

Time Required: This will depend upon two factors: (1) how much of your prior learning can be documented, and (2) how much time and effort you can invest each quarter. Students enroll for a minimum of three quarters to several years.

82

Mississippi

Department of Independent Study
University of Southern Mississippi
Southern Station, Box #5056
Hattiesburg, Mississippi 39401

(601) 266-4206

Background: Although no degree is available through correspondence and/or independent study, a number of courses are available that may enable the student to complete an external degree with another institution. The student must always check to make certain that the courses are acceptable and transferable to the institution awarding the degree. This may sound a bit obvious, but you would be surprised at the number of people who make this basic mistake.

Admission: Open-entry, open-exit. Admission to independent study does not constitute admission to the university.

Degrees Awarded: None through independent study, although up to one-fourth of a degree at the University of Southern Mississippi may be earned through independent study and/or extension.

Tuition: A fee of $27 for a one-semester-hour course; $54 for a two-semester-hour course; $81 for a three-semester-hour course. High school fees are $39 per one-half unit.

Study Program: Following a course syllabus, the student prepares written assignments. A final examination is required.

Credit for Life Experience: No.

Time Required: One month is the minimum time in which a course may be completed, and one year is the maximum.

Missouri

Clayton University
Suite #404
7710 Carondelet Avenue
Clayton, Missouri 63105

(314) 727-6100

Background: Clayton University was founded in 1972 to serve the mid-career adult. The program is self-paced and credit is offered for experiential learning. No contact with the campus is required. In the words of one Clayton University brochure: "We welcome the opportunity to work with businesses, school systems, and governments to set up in-service programs leading to a degree. If you would like to develop a program in a special area of interest for your organization we would be happy to discuss it with you." This institution is authorized by the state of Missouri to grant degrees and is accredited by the U.S. Department of Education.

Admission: Open, as least as this observer read their literature.

Degrees Offered: A.A.; B.A.; M.A.; Ph.D.

Tuition: $3000 per academic year; $300 graduation fee.

Study Program: Clayton does "not offer correspondence study, or day or evening classes. We do offer an in-service, work-based program tailored for you by Clayton University and your faculty committee to meet your goals and objectives."

Credit for Life Experience: Yes. In the words of a letter to a prospective student: "To help you determine your present level of accomplishments, Clayton University offers you a preliminary assessment of your prior learning and experience. This service costs $25 and allows you to determine approximately how much credit you have already earned through experience, formal courses, and other learning activities."

Time Required: "Through the appropriate presentation of one's educational and work background, we believe that a legitimate degree can be earned relatively expeditiously." To paraphrase their promotional literature, since many highly qualified people were only a dissertation—or similar project—away from a degree, Clayton University exists to aid them.

Columbia College
10th and Rogers Streets
Columbia, Missouri 65216

(314) 449-0531

Background: Columbia has many adjunct programs operating at military bases, but there is no correspondence instruction. Contact with an adjunct instructor and class attendance are required. Columbia is accredited by the North Central Association of Colleges and Secondary Schools; also a member of the Servicemember's Opportunity Colleges. Nor is experiential credit official until the student completes 12 semester hours with a 2.00 GPA or better.

Degrees Awarded: A.A.; B.A. in (1) Individual Studies, (2) Business Administration, (3) Psychology, (4) History/Government, (5) Criminal Justice Administration; or the Bachelor of Science in (1) Administration of Justice, (2) Business Administration, (3) Public Administration.

Study Program: Eight-week "minimesters" meeting a minimum of 40 "clock contact hours." Six credit hours may be earned each eight weeks. Not all degree programs will necessarily be available at all locations. Normal university requirements apply to attendance, academic probation, graduation, etc.

Admissions: High school diploma, the General Educational Development Test, transcript of successful previous college work, or "honorable military service."

Credit for Life Experience: Columbia is a member of the Council for Advancement of Experiential Learning, and up to 45 semester hours of credit may be earned for experiential learning. Military service and training do not count. Also the College Level Entrance Program, United States Armed Forces Institute and Defense Activity for Non-Traditional Education Support may be utilized to establish academic credit by examination. There is a $100 fee for portfolio evaluation.

Tuition: Admission fee of $15. A fee of $75 per semester hour, $225 for average course. This does not include books or other fees. A $15 graduation fee.

Time Required: This would depend solely upon the student, his or her motivation, and the amount of experiential or examination credit.

Center for Independent Study
University of Missouri—Columbia
1030 Whitten Hall
Columbia, Missouri 65211

(314) 882-6287

Background: This program has offered correspondence courses since 1911, and there were 14,350 new enrollments in independent study during 1980–81. Thus, they are experienced and know the trials and tribulations of the adult learner. High school courses are offered, as is a nontraditional program in agriculture. This program also offers the Computer Assisted Lesson Service, which is "unique among university correspondence programs." Certain courses "provide computer responses to the lessons that students submit." "Not only are the computer responses to each programmed lesson returned very promptly, but the computer feedback itself, which is prepared by the professor or high school instructor who designed the course, contains special instructional commentary and feedback." Approximately 165 computer-assisted courses are offered. The university is a member of the University of Mid-America, a consortium of eleven midwestern universities that went out of business because of lack of funding on October 1, 1982. Its various functions are to be detailed to another unit. This had not been accomplished as this book goes to press. Graduate credit is available, which is not the general case in such lifelong correspondence programs. Graduate credit is "awarded only to students who have been admitted to a university graduade school and who have satisfactorily completed a course designated as graduate level."

Admission: Open to anyone, but you must be formally admitted to the university to receive credit, which is standard for most of the institutions herein. Priority is afforded to those students who have about 50–60 hours for admission into the nontraditional agricultural program.

Degrees Awarded: None awarded solely through independent study.

Tuition: $42.50 per semester hour for undergraduates; $46.75 per semester hour for graduate credits.

Study Program: A study guide, textbooks, all the typical materials of routine correspondence education are here waiting for you.

Credit for Life Experience: No.

Time Required: You are allowed nine months to complete a course with one three-month extension possible. For your edification, they estimate about six months as an average completion time for a three-hour course. "Only under extraordinary circumstances could a student complete an Independent Study course in less than six weeks, therefore you should not enroll with this expectation."

Stephens College
P.O. Box #2083
Columbia, Missouri 65215

(314) 442-2211, ext. 544

Background: Founded in 1833, Stephens' residential program is for women only. Stephens' College Without Walls, Liberal Studies Seminar was first offered in 1971. Fifteen seminars are offered annually through the United States, together making up the college-without-walls program. During their reaccreditation in 1978, the North Central Association of Colleges and Secondary Schools cited Stephens' program as "an innovative effort of an expressly imaginative sort."

Admission: Applicants must be 23 years or older. The Liberal Studies Seminar is required, during which the student must prove her capacity for this program. It is worth one credit hour. All transcripts must be forwarded to the Admissions Office. Two letters of recommendation are required.

Degrees Awarded: B.A.; Bachelor of Fine Arts; A.A.

Tuition: The tuition for each guided-study course in $310.00, and the student should figure a minimum cost of $3500.

Credit for Life Experience: Yes, through the preparation of a portfolio. Their catalog states: "Students who enter SCWW with fewer than 30 courses are strongly encouraged to consider the possibility of this option for earning credit." All sorts of life experiences may be submitted for credit evaluation, such as work, family life, hobbies, travel and "course work from nonaccredited colleges and universities." These credits can be used to meet degree requirements, but you must still take a minimum of ten courses with Stephens. Testing via CLEP may also be used to establish credit. Professional training from noncollegiate institutions may be assessed for college credits.

Study Program: Most students complete the majority of the program via independent study. Independent study can be "guided" or by "contract." Guided study involves a course structured by the instructor. Contract study is "designed cooperatively between the instructor and the student." Classroom instruction at Stephens and other selected locations is available as an alternative.

Time Required to Complete Degree: The student must complete ten courses with the Stephens faculty.

Park College School for Community Education
818 Grand Avenue
Kansas City, Missouri 64106

(816) 741-2000

Director of Portfolio
Park College—Scarritt Building
818 Grand Avenue—8th Avenue
Kansas City, Missouri 64106

(816) 842-6182

Background: Park College is an independent institution affiliated with the Reorganized Church of Jesus Christ of Latter Day Saints. Park College has resident programs operating at a number of military bases in the United States. Park also has a portfolio program for the mature student who has already completed a significant number of college credits.

   The School for Community Education is a Servicemember's Opportunity College. This provides members of the military the "opportunity to complete Park College degree requirements by means of course work from other institutions taken after the candidate has completed a minimum of twenty-four hours with the School for Community Education toward a bachelor's degree, or fifteen hours toward an associate's degree."

Degrees Awarded: A.A. and B.A.

Admission: High school diploma or GED. Students will be allowed to transfer from another institution with less than a 2.0 GPA, on a probationary basis.

Requirements: For A.A.—60 credit hours and a 2.0 GPA or better; for B.A.—120 credit hours, a 2.0 GPA or better, plus no less than 30 hours of upper-division work and "no less than 24 graded Park College earned-credit hours needed for the residency period."

Study Program: There are three methods for study through the School for Community Education: The Portfolio Plan Program, MetroPark, and the Military Resident System.

Credit for Life Experience: Yes, through Portfolio appraisal.

Tuition: A fee of $60 per credit hour through the Military Resident Center System and MetroPark. The twelve-month Portfolio Program, consisting of 24–36 credit hours is a total of $2530. Any time over a twelve-month program is "prorated at the twelve-month tuition rate."

Time Required: At least two semesters, depending upon the status of the student upon entry into the program, and his or her prior learning.

Webster College
190 East Lockwood
Webster Groves, Missouri 63119

(314) 968-7090

Background: Located in suburban suburban St. Louis, this independent, coeducational institution has about 1500 undergraduates, and 4000 graduate students. Beginning in the fall of 1982, Dimension 3 will be offered beginning in August 1982, to "allow working adults to earn credits toward a degree." Dimension 3 consists of "a combination of TV lectures, a weekly seminar held at a convenient location and a once-a-month weekend conference." Tuition for Dimension 3 is $73 per credit hour.

Degrees Awarded: B.A., B.S., Master of Arts and Master of Music.

Admission: High school diploma, a transcript of the student's academic record, SAT or ACT scores.

Requirements: 128 credit hours, 30 credit hours earned at Webster College.

Study Program: The study may work toward a degree through a number of methods including credit for life experience, Individualized Learning Experiences, and evening or weekend course work.

Credit for Life Experience: Yes, based upon a portfolio that demonstrates prior learning. Also, credit by examination, as well as credit for certain military and business training.

Tuition: A fee of $73 per credit hour for off-campus programs such as Dimension 3. Regular tuition is $122 per credit hour.

Time Required: At least one year.

Nebraska

Independent Study Department
Nebraska Center for Continuing Education
33rd and Holdrege Streets
University of Nebraska—Lincoln
Lincoln, Nebraska 68583-0900

(402) 472-1926
(402) 472-1392

Background: About 100 courses are offered by this state-supported school. Continuing Education Units are available, as is graduate credit.

Admission: Open-entry, open-exit. Admission to correspondence study does not constitute admission to the university.

Tuition: A fee of $32 per semester hour.

Degrees Awarded: None through correspondence study.

Study Program: Routine correspondence study. Examinations are required.

Credit for Life Experience: No.

Time Required: One year is allowed to complete a course.

New Jersey

**Academic Programs for
Non-traditional Students
Bloomfield College
Bloomfield, New Jersey 07003**

(201) 748-9000

Background: Bloomfield's roots go back to 1868. This college offers programs leading to the traditional liberal arts and sciences degrees, as well as career-oriented
degrees in business and nursing. Bloomfield also offers a variety of Certificate Programs in: Accounting, Communications; Industrial/Organizational Psychology;
Marketing; Personnel; Materials Management. Another positive feature of Bloomfield is the Contract Program, which allows the student to structure a "cross disciplinary set of major requirements which will take the place of a traditional disciplinary
major."

Admission: High school diploma or GED.

Tuition: A fee of $402 per course; $1230 for evening, weekend and the summer session,
which covers three courses. Senior citizens pay 50 percent of the tuition rate if they
are taking the course for credit. Those auditing a course on a noncredit basis pay
$15 per course, if space is available.

Degrees Awarded: B.A.; B.S.

Study Program: Evening and weekend courses, as well as Independent Study, and CLEP.

Credit for Life Experience: Yes. "The maximum award of credit is sixteen course equiv-
alents for Life Assessment and CLEP credit."

Time Required: At least two semesters, depending upon the background of the student entering Bloomfield.

External Degree Program
Caldwell College
Caldwell, New Jersey 07006

(201) 228-4424, ext. 216

Background: The External Degree Program is open to students 23 or older. Campus contact is required one weekend each semester. The rest of the program is self-paced and external.

Admission: High school diploma or GED, and applicants must be 23 or older.

Tuition: A fee of $115 per credit hour.

Degrees Awarded: B.A.; B.S.; Bachelor of Fine Arts.

Study Program: The student carries one to five courses per semester. Only one weekend per semester of campus contact is required.

Credit for Life Experience: Yes, through portfolio assessment, and through CLEP.

Time Required: At least one year.

Continuing Education
Centenary College
400 Jefferson Street
Hackettstown, New Jersey 07840

(201) 852-1400

Background: Centenary is essentially a private woman's college. Contact with this campus/program is required. Centenary also offers an Individualized Studies program that results in a B.A. Those interested in this option must set forth their plan prior to their junior year.

Admission: Open to adults 23 or older.

92   **Degrees Offered:**   Associate and Baccalaureate.

Tuition: A fee of $98 per semester hour for the first course and $88 per semester hour for 4–11 credits, for the Weekend and Evening College. The tuition for senior citizens is $49 per semester hour.

Study Program: There is also a limited amount of Independent Study available. No more than eight credits may be applied to an Associate's degree. "The maximum number of credits applicable towards a Bachelor's degree will be determined by the nature of the student's program."

Credit for Life Experience: Yes. A maximum of 32 Life Learning credits may be applied to an Associate degree. 64 credits of Life Learning may be applied to a Baccalaureate degree.

Time Required: At least one year, and probably longer.

Office of Continuing Education
Ramapo College
505 Ramapo Valley Road
Mahwah, New Jersey 07430

(201) 825-2800, ext. 213

Background: Founded in 1969, Ramapo is a four-year state college; 21 academic majors are offered. Persons over 65 may audit courses free on a space-available basis. Contact with the campus is required, as there is no external-degree program.

Admission: High school diploma.

Degrees Awarded: B.A., B.S.

Tuition: One semester hour is $35.45 for New Jersey residents and $55.45 for out-of-state residents.

Study Program: Applicants must complete 120 semester hours.

Credit for Life Experience: Yes. Up to 75 semester hours. The "75 credit limit" refers to the combination of credits transferred from other colleges or given for CLEP, PEP, TECEP, or PLEX (Prior Learning Experience Program).

Time Required: At least three semesters, since Ramapo accepts a maximum of 75 transfer credits.

Thomas A. Edison State College
The Kelsey Building
101 West State Building
Trenton, New Jersey 08625

(609) 984-1100

Background: This institution is the New Jersey State College for external degrees. Edison was founded in 1972 and received full accreditation from the Middle States Association of Colleges and Schools in 1977. Edison is also a member of the

> Committee on Institutional Cooperation
> Independent Study Project
> 990 Grove Street
> Evanston, Illinois 60201

The committee is composed of six state universities that offer correspondence degrees.

Degrees Awarded: This external, nontraditional program offers a B.A. degree. More interesting is the Bachelor of Sciences degree in Human or Technical Services. According to their literature, this degree is "designed to meet the educational and professional needs of mid-career adults in a wide variety of human and technical services fields. The degree includes both a liberal arts component and an individually-tailored specialization. Some of the specializations in Human Services are Art Therapy, Community Services, Counseling Services . . . ," and so forth, through a wide variety of possibilities. The Bachelor of Science in Business Administration is also of considerable interest to the "adult who has acquired a college-level business administration background through experience or independent study." The major point is that the student is not confined to the usual nontraditional liberal arts major.

Admissions: In their own words: "The College is open to all, regardless of age, previous education, or residency."

Credit for Experiential Learning: As with many nontraditional institutions, Thomas A. Edison College offers college credit for experiential learning. Edison's brochure states that it is possible to "earn a substantial number of credits toward a college degree through this method." It is worth noting that while Edison State is open in its admissions policy, some 11,000 adult students have enrolled and over 2500 degrees have been awarded. Since there are currently about 4500 students in the program, one may deduce that it is not a pushover program or an automatic degree.

Edison participates in the Program on Noncollegiate Sponsored Instruction, a program of the American Council on Education. The purpose of this program is to "help people get academic credit for learning they have acquired outside the sponsorship of colleges and universities by providing educational institutions with reliable information to use in making decisions on credit awards."

94

To receive credit the student must prove that he or she knows the subject. This is done by preparing a portfolio that consists of documents, papers, and other evidence that the applicant knows the subject matter. Portfolio assessment can begin at any time. Credit based upon portfolio assessment is awarded in two to six months. New Jersey residents pay $75 plus $12 per credit hour attempted for portfolio assessment. There is a fee of $125 for out-of-state students, plus $18.00 per credit hour attempted.

Credit by Examination also allows the student to establish college credits under a variety of different programs. The Thomas Edison State College Examination Program, the College-Level Examination Program, the ACT-Proficiency Examination Program, and the Advanced Placement Program are testing programs offered at various centers in New Jersey.

New Mexico

Independent Study
The University of New Mexico
Division of Continuing Education
and Community Services
805 Yale Boulevard, NE
Albuquerque, New Mexico 87131

Background: Founded in 1928, and a member of the National University Extension Association. No graduate credit is offered. These credits may be used for teacher certification.

Admission: Open to high school graduates or anyone over 21. Enrollment for external courses does not constitute acceptance to the university.

Degrees Awarded: None. However, up to thirty hours of independent credit awarded by this program may be applied to a degree at the University of New Mexico.

Tuition: A fee of $30.00 per semester hour.

Study Program: Normal correspondence methods with regular examinations.

Credit for Life Experience: No.

Time Required: A maximum of one year is allowed to complete a course.

New York

Regents External Degree
College Proficiency Examination Programs
Cultural Education Center
Albany, New York 12230

(518) 474-3703
(518) 473-8957 (Nursing degrees)

Background: This degree is not to be confused with any other nontraditional studies offered by New York colleges and universities. The Regents External Degree was established in 1972, and more than 15,000 people have earned them. The program is accredited by the Middle States Association of Colleges and Schools. There is no residency requirement, nor is there any classroom or correspondence instruction available.

[*Regents Credit Bank:* For $125 *anyone* can have "all records of college-level work evaluated according to consistent academic standards." Transcripts from this credit bank are used for educational, military, and for employment purposes. Those who enroll in the External Degree automatically receive this service.]

Admission: Open to anyone, anywhere.

Tuition: There is a $175 enrollment fee; $100 Annual Records Maintenance Fee; $300 Special Assessment Fee.

Degrees Awarded: A.A.; A.S.; A.S. (nursing); Associate in Applied Science (Nursing); B.S. (Nursing); B.A.; B.S.; B.S. (Business).

Study Program: A student may take college courses from any accredited college or university. This flexibility would allow a student to collect his or her credits through the Regents Credit Bank and wrap up missing course work at nearly any college or university. Such individualized instruction is the quintessence of nontraditional education. Credits are also earned by examination, military-education programs, courses offered in business, industry, government and police agencies, and the Federal Aviation Agency and Civil Aeronautics Administration.

Credit for Experiential Learning: Yes. Also, all Regents External Degrees may be earned by examination.

Time Required: Since a degree can be earned based upon credit for life experience and by examination this is potentially an expeditious program.

Department of Continuing Education
Mercy College
555 Broadway
Dobbs Ferry, New York 10522

(914) 693-7600

Background: Mercy College's roots go back to 1950, when it was founded as a junior college by the Roman Catholic Sisters of Mercy. Mercy is a private, independent, coeducational, nonsectarian, four-year institution. They offer Lifelong Learning for adults, professional-development programs, and certificate programs. Their literature states that about sixty percent of their students are between the ages of 25 and 60. Contact with the campus for these programs is required. There are also campuses at Yorktown, Peekskill, White Plains, Yonkers, and the Bronx.

Admission: High school diploma or GED.

Tuition: A fee of $95 per semester hour; $2850 for full-time students carrying 30 semester hours per year.

Degrees Awarded: A.A.; B.A.; B.S.

Study Program: Routine college study. There are also Independent Study projects, tutorial courses, credit by examination.

Credit for Life Experience: Yes, up to fifteen credits may be earned for life experience.

Time Required: At least two semesters.

University Without Walls at New College
Hofstra University
206 Weed Hall
Hempstead, New York 11550

(516) 560-3651

Background: This program is a competence-based, liberal arts, B.A. program for those who cannot spend much time on campus. Contact with campus is required, since the student must satisfy a "Collegia" requirement. Eight Collegia seminars are held each year, on Saturdays. There are two residence periods, which are held on Saturdays and Sundays. A student must attend six of these sessions annually. This is a flexible and individualized program for the mature student.

Degrees Awarded: B.A.

Admission: High school diploma or GED equivalent. *If* you have taken the SAT, ACT, or CLEP tests, have these scores forwarded to the admissions department. You must provide the admissions department with two or three personal references. Other requirements include "a tentative outline of the applicant's proposed program of study and possible modes of learning which may be employed in an individualized program"; a biographical essay covering your educational, work and intellectual developments; and an on-campus interview. No less than one-quarter of the student's degree program must be completed at Hofstra.

Credit for Life Experience: Yes, through portfolio assessment. Credit is also established through CLEP, etc.

Study Program: The student, in conjunction with a faculty advisor, develops a Graduation Plan. This plan shows how the "student's prior learning and learning modes satisfy each requirement." The student must also design and prepare a Final Project which is generally related to the student's "depth concentration."

Tuition: Full-contract tuition, $1060; half-contract tuition, $530.

Time Required: At least two semesters.

**Admissions Department
Friends World College
Huntington, New York 11743**

(516) 549-1102

Background: Founded in 1965, this is a truly nontraditional liberal arts college, with Quaker roots. It does not offer any correspondence courses and is definitely oriented toward the learner seeking full-time involvement in his or her education. The international program offers the opportunity to "live, study and work in two or more other cultures while earning the B.A. degree." The student designs an "individual program" based on "personal interests and goals." Students will travel to another country for a significant portion of their studies. Friends World College has regional centers around the globe. Many will be unable to participate in this program because of the time and travel involved, but it does provide a quintessentially nontraditional education. Younger students and parents with children nearing college age might consider this program as an alternative.

Admission: Open.

Degrees Offered: B.A.

Tuition: A fee of $1900 per semester in tuition *plus* $3885 for room and board, field travel, books and supplies, and personal expenses, in North America for 1981–1982. "Even with such worldwide learning, average costs for a full twelve month program are comparable to expenses for a regular academic year at a typical independent liberal art college.

"Financial aid is available for those with proven need, and over two-thirds of FWC students receive such assistance."

Study Program: The " 'instructional method' is a series of carefully planned individual learning experiences—field study projects—in a succession of cultural settings."

Credit for Life Experience: Yes, in every sense of the word, but college credit is not awarded for any knowledge you have amassed before entry into this program.

Time Required: Four years and, from the looks of the program and the philosophy undergirding it, worth every minute of the time required.

City University of New York
Room #1403
33 West 42nd Street
New York, New York 10036

(212) 790-4558

Background: An external-degree program was established in 1971 to permit "mature and highly motivated students with a clear idea of their own educational and career objectives to design their own academic programs." Under the guidance of a faculty committee, the student designs a totally individualized study program.

Admission: You must be accepted into CUNY and earn or transfer in 15 semester hours before being admitted into this program. A minimum GPA of 2.5 is required.

Degrees Awarded: B.A. or B.S.

Tuition: A fee of $462.50 per semester for New York residents; $712.50 for out-of-state full-time students.

Study Program: This program allows the student considerable latitude and flexibility. This is a low classroom-requirement program of only 15 semester hours.

Credit for Life Experience: Yes, up to 15 semester hours may be granted for experiential learning.

Time Required: At least 30 semester hours must be completed in this program. Also, at least "15 credits of the 30 credit residency MUST be earned in the classroom."

Dominican College of Blauvelt
Western Highway
Orangeburg, New York 10962

(914) 359-7800

Background: Founded in 1952, this is a four-year, liberal arts college. Several professional programs are offered, in addition to the liberal arts offerings. Contact with the campus is required.

Admission: Two letters of recommendation and one's previous educatonal transcripts.

Tuition: A fee of $85 per credit; 1–5 credits, $40; 6–8 credits, $55; 9–11 credits, $70; 12–18 credits, $85.

Degrees Awarded: B.A.; B.S.; B.S. in Education; B.S. in Nursing; Bachelor of Professional Studies; A.A.

Study Program: The adult may pursue studies through weekend, evening, Independent Study, CLEP, and credit for previous learning. One must still complete thirty semester hours in residence.

Credit for Life Experience: Yes, up to 30 semester hours may be earned through portfolio presentation.

Time Required: Since a minimum of 30 semester hours must be completed at Dominican, the student must expect to spend at least one year.

School of Adult Education
Marist College
Poughkeepsie, New York 12601

(914) 471-3240, ext. 221

Background: This is a flexible program for both graduate and undergraduate credit. Senior citizens and alumni may audit any course for a fee of $10. Contact with the campus is required.

Admission: Routine process. Applicants must show capability for the work and meet with an admissions counselor before enrolling for any courses. Graduate students must be admitted into a specific program.

Degrees Awarded: B.S.; B.A.; M.B.A.; Master of Public Administration; Master of Arts in Counseling Community Psychology.

Tuition: A fee of $140 per credit hour for undergraduates; $155 per hour for graduate students.

Study Program: Self-paced independent study, "mini-mesters," proficiency-testing programs, credit for life experience, and formal classroom lectures.

Credit for Life Experience: Yes, up to 30 credit hours by "taking standardized or departmental proficiency exams, by performing a learned skill or by preparing a written presentation."

Time Required: You may transfer in up to 90 semester hours from four-year schools, which means one year at best.

Center for Distance Learning
Empire State College
State University of New York
2 Union Avenue
Saratoga Springs, New York 12866

(518) 587-2100

Background: Established in 1971. Empire State College's "mission is to bring high quality undergraduate programs" to New Yorkers for whom traditional education is not feasible. Accredited by the Middle States Association of Schools and Colleges. (Do not confuse the Center for Distance Learning with the Regents External Degree option.) ESC offers its programs at 35 locations throughout New York state. Please note: "Students having telephone numbers outside the State may enroll if they are willing to accept collect calls from tutors approximately once every two weeks."

Admission: High school diploma.

Degrees Awarded: Associate in Arts, Associate in Science, Bachelor of Science, and Bachelor of Professional Studies. A bachelor's degree in Fire Service Administration is available to residents of New York, Pennsylvania, Vermont, New Hampshire, Massachusetts, Connecticut, Maine, and Rhode Island.

Study Program: Empire State College established the Center for Distance Learning to serve out-of-state students and those who because of work, handicaps, etc., cannot attend. "The Center offers a structured degree program, based on a specific set of courses, and using educational materials especially designed for those students unable to attend regularly scheduled classes." Students seeking an A.A. or A.S. degree must complete 24 credit hours while enrolled at ESC. Those pursuing a bachelor's degree must successfully attain 32 semester hours of credit. There is also an Independent Study program that requires a degree of residency.

Credit for Experiential Learning: Yes, credit is awarded provided it fulfills part of the degree. The student prepares a portfolio of prior learning. You must be enrolled at Empire State for evaluation.

Tuition: A fee of $525.00 for New York residents; $875.00 for out-of-state students.

Time Required: At least two semesters, probably longer.

Skidmore College
University Without Walls
Saratoga Springs, New York 12866

(518) 584-5000

Background: In the words of its brochure, "SUWW does not offer courses, one of its main functions is to help students identify or create educational resources and to construct substantial baccalaureate degree programs. It believes that resources for college-level learning exist within a diversity of experiences—in the home, at work, through internships and apprenticeships, at more than one college, in tutorial situations, and by involvement in the community." This is an exceptional institution for the adult learner, for it allows you to structure your education. Even better, it is accredited by the Middle States Association of Colleges and Secondary Schools. "SUWW graduates have found their unique educational program to be widely accepted for entrance into graduate schools."

Degrees Awarded: Bachelor of Arts or Bachelor of Science.

Admission: Open-entry, open-exit. An interview process is required. Also, a narrative autobiography, two letters of recommendation, and a detailed explanation of your reasons for wanting to attend. Official transcripts must be forwarded to the admissions office.

Requirements: An extraordinarily flexible program, with "no specified number of experiences which the student must undertake at any given time." The student and instructor "evaluate" each learning experience upon its completion.

Study Program: By the end of the first year the student, with the assistance of the advisor, develops a degree plan. A SUWW faculty committee reviews this proposal, which is based upon your interests and goals. To conclude the program, each student must prepare a final project, yet what the project consists of is flexible, pending faculty approval.

Tuition: This will depend upon the amount of time the student takes to complete the program. Tuition is $800 per calendar year. There are associated fees for various faculty evaluations, and so forth. It is reasonable to estimate about $2500 to $4000 for tuition. Incidentally, you are billed tuition each year on the anniversary of your enrollment. If you graduate within the first quarter of that year, Skidmore will refund three-fourths of that year's tuition. An eminently fair policy, deserving commendation.

Time Required: This is an open-entry, open-exit program. All factors considered, it is at least a one-year program under the best of circumstances, and more likely two to as many as four years. However, any applicant should always make direct contact with an institution as the next step after reading this description. Your background may permit you to move more rapidly through a program such as this.

Independent Study Degree Programs
Syracuse University, University College
610 E. Fayette Street
Syracuse, New York 13202

(315) 423-3284

Background: Syracuse, an urban and independent school more than a century old, has offered "adults an opportunity to earn degrees through limited residence and independent study since 1966." "Week-long residencies scheduled three times a year (MBA, BA, and BS) or one two-week residency scheduled annually (MFA and MSSc) are the core" of this program. These residencies are required. For undergraduates a maximum of 90 semester hours may be transferred to the program. If you can attend the residencies and are not in a rush, these seem solid programs well worth the effort.

Admissions: Standards depend upon the program, but they are somewhat tighter than other programs. One should take the appropriate Scholastic Aptitude Tests and have transcripts forwarded to the registrar.

Degrees Awarded: Five degrees are available on a low-residential and/or independent basis: Master of Business Administration; Master of Fine Arts (emphasis in Advertising Design or Illustration; Master of Social Science; Bachelor of Arts (Liberal Studies); B.S. in Business Administration.

Tuition: The 1980–81 tuition was $95 per hour for undergraduate credit; $150 per hour for graduate credit. There is also the cost of the residencies.

Study Program: Students attend a residency that enables them to plan for the next set of studies under the program.

Credit for Life Experience: Yes, but the policy varies from program to program.

Time Required: An estimated maximum of seven years, if you are "starting from scratch." About one to two years seems average.

104

Nevada

Continuing Education
Independent Study
University of Nevada—Reno
Reno, Nevada 89557

(702) 784-1110

Background: Routine undergraduate correspondence study; no graduate credit is offered via correspondence. No fully external degree is possible.

Admission: Applicants must be 18 years of age or older or have proof of high school graduation. Essentially an open-admission situation.

Degrees Awarded: Up to 60 semester hours of correspondence study may be applied toward a University of Nevada degree.

Tuition: A fee of $31.00 per credit hour.

Study Program: You may take up to two correspondence courses at a time. Midterm and final examinations are required.

Credit for Life Experience: No.

Time Required: One year is allowed to complete a course with one six-month extension. You may not complete a three-credit course in less than five weeks.

North Carolina

Independent Study by Extension
University of North Carolina
Abernethy Hall 002A
Chapel Hill, North Carolina 27514

(919) 962-1106

Background: This program represents a consortium of eight institutions within the University of North Carolina.

Admission: Open, but admission to independent study does not constitute admission to the University of North Carolina.

Degrees Awarded: None through this independent-study program.

Tuition: A 2-semester-hour course, $80; a 3-semester-hour course, $120; a 4-semester-hour course, $160.

Study Program: Usual correspondence form of study. A final examination is required of those who seek credit for the course.

Credit for Life Experience: No.

Time Required: There is a one-year time limit on correspondence courses.

North Dakota

Department of Correspondence Study
University of North Dakota
Box #8277, University Station
Grand Forks, North Dakota 58202

(701) 777-3044

Background: This is a typical correspondence-study program that will not lead directly to a degree. Correspondence courses may be taken concurrently with campus courses.

Degrees Awarded: None directly through this program, although its course offerings may be used to supplement your work elsewhere. It is the responsibility of the student to make certain that any correspondence work is applicable to his or her degree or certification goals.

Admissions: Open.

Courses Offered: Accounting, Business Law, Economics, Graphics, Marketing, Management, Mathematics, and Religious Studies, among others.

Credit for Life Experience: No.

Study Program: Two courses may be taken at a time, which must be completed within one year.

Tuition: A fee of $26.00 per semester hour.

Time Required: Information not available.

Ohio

Ohio University
Independent Study
302 Tupper Hall
Athens, Ohio 45701

(614) 594-6721
(800) 282-4408 (in-state only)

Background: The Ohio University Independent Program was established in 1923 and is accredited by the North Central Association of Colleges and Secondary Schools.

Degrees Awarded: The External Student Program can lead to an A.A. or baccalaureate degree (Bachelor of General Studies). The Ohio University lifelong-study bulletin states: "While it is possible to structure a degree solely through independent study offerings in some areas, it may be necessary to take certain courses . . ." elsewhere.

Admissions: Open to "all who can profit from it and formal admission to the University is not required for enrollment."

Credit for Life Experience: Credit may be established by examination at a cost of $13.00 per quarter hour. Credit may also be granted for Military Service Schools, and Technical Colleges. Ohio University also grants credit for life experience. For further information contact:

Adult Learning Services
309 Tupper Hall

Credit for prior Experience is limited to 24 hours for an associate degree, 48 hours for a bachelor's degree.

Study Program: Most courses require a midterm and final examination. Students not living in Ohio can arrange to take these tests at another college or university.

Tuition: A fee of $23.00 per quarter hour* for undergraduate Independent Study correspondence courses. One graduate course is available at $29.00 per quarter hour. Credit by Examination costs $13.00/quarter hour.

Time Required: This is something of a wild card that will depend upon the student's background. At least two semesters, in all likelihood.

*The Quarter-Hour System:
    1.5 quarter hours = 1 semester hour
    3.0 quarter hours = 2 semester hours
    4.5 quarter hours = 3 semester hours
    6.0 quarter hours = 4 semester hours
    7.5 quarter hours = 5 semester hours

The Union for Experimenting Colleges and Universities
P.O. Box #85315
Provident Bank Building
Cincinnati, Ohio 45201

Background: The Union has offices in several major cities and operates a thoroughly respectable program of high caliber. This institution offers an interdisciplinary, self-directed Ph.D. The Union was chartered in Ohio in 1971. The Union is a Candidate for Accreditation by the North Central Association of Colleges and Schools. (A list of the various accrediting agencies has been included as Appendix B for those who may have questions about the legitimacy of many of the programs mentioned in this book. These agencies are in a position to definitively answer any questions you may have.)

Degrees Awarded: Bachelor of Arts, Bachelor of Science, and the Doctor of Philosophy.

Locations Where Programs are Offered: Undergraduate programs are available only in Cincinnati. The doctorate is also available in Washington, D.C., New Orleans, and San Francisco.

Admission: "Application to the Union Graduate School should be made only by candidates who clearly cannot obtain the kind of advanced training they require within more conventional programs." In their own words, "The admissions process is exacting," sometimes requiring more than a month and occasionally involving a personal interview. The Union program is clearly no pushover leading to a worthless piece of paper.

Interestingly and importantly, a Master's Degree is not always necessary for acceptance into a doctoral program. This means that a student can earn a doctorate in a shorter period of time.

Requirements/The Program: The Union offers an interdisciplinary Ph.D. program. The student "develops a program to suit his or her own needs, strengths, and opportunities." With the appropriate guidance from a tutor/mentor/advisor/professor.

Credit for Life Experience: Yes.

Study Program: In their own succinct words: "Each learner prepares a Project Demonstrating Excellence (PDE) which may resemble a dissertation or, since the Union Graduate School concept is broad enough to include other types of products, a publishable book, a unified series of essays or articles, a documented project of social change or innovation, outstanding creations in poetry, media presentation, painting, or a musical composition. Regardless of form, the PDE must represent a significant contribution to our society and culture." As a self-devised and self-directed program, the student has many nontraditional opportunities to learn.

Tuition: A fee of $3600 per year, payable quarterly at the rate of $900.

Time Required: "Persons holding a Master's degree are required to spend at least eighteen months in the program before being awarded the Ph.D. degree." The would-be student should be aware that the Union's program does require a certain amount of contact with the faculty and other students. Students must attend 15 days of seminars before final completion of the doctoral requirements.

Capital University
University Without Walls
2199 E. Main Street
Columbus, Ohio 43209

(513) 228-5006

Background: Capital University was chartered in 1850. Capital UWW is part of the College of Arts and Sciences. Affiliated with the Lutheran Church. Contact with the campus is required, unlike other "university without walls" programs.

Admission: Applicants must be at least 21 years of age; have a personal interview; high school diploma or GED; two reference letters.

Degrees Offered: Bachelor of General Studies.

Tuition: A fee of $115 per credit hour on a part-time basis; $1200 per 12-semester-hour term full-time, or $3600 annually; $345 for the Prior Learning Portfolio class.

Study Program: The program is based upon contract learning, "a written agreement between the student and faculty member, stating mutual expectations for the duration of the learning project." The contract sets forth what the student will learn, how, what proof the student will offer of having learned the material, and the evaluation criteria that are to be utilized.

Credit for Life Experience: Yes, through the preparation of a Prior Learning Portfolio. Capital will also generally accept all credit earned at accredited institutions.

Time Required: A total of 124 semester hours are required for graduation. They require a minimum enrollment of one academic year.

Director of Admissions
Garfield Senior College
Painesville, Ohio 44077

(216) 352-3361

Background: Garfield is one of 30 senior colleges in the United States, offering the final two years of schooling for junior college graduates. Most of Garfield's students are employed full or part-time, which means that this school is attuned to the needs of adult learners. Their literature states that "Garfield's liberal credit transfer policy is a great asset." Contact with the program is required, but evening and weekend classes are offered as well. The program allows for independent study, internships and credit for experiential learning. A special program called New Dimensions is available to women who are over 25 and who have been out of school for five or more years.

Admission: Degree from a junior college or a minimum of 45 semester hours with a 2.0 GPA or better.

Degrees Awarded: B.A.; B.S.

Tuition: A fee of $85 per semester hour for undergraduate courses; $95 per hour for graduate courses.

Study Program: All pedagogical methods are employed at this institution.

Credit for Life Experience: Yes, through portfolio assessment.

110   **Time Required:**   At least two semesters.

Division of Lifelong Learning
Heidelberg College
Tiffin, Ohio 44883

(419) 448-2800

Background: Founded in 1850, Heidelberg is an independent, liberal arts institution operated by the United Church of Christ. They have a number of programs for the adult student through their Weekend College, which meets every other weekend.

Degrees Awarded: B.A., B.S.

Admission: Admission is based upon "(1) motivation and (2) the ability to do college work." High school diploma, and transcripts of any college work.

Requirements: A total of 120 semester hours is required for graduation.

Study Program: The "Weekend College meets every other weekend throughout the fall, spring, and summer terms. Classes are held on Friday evenings, Saturday mornings and afternoons, and Sunday mornings." The student may take up to four courses in the fall and spring, and three in summer. This will allow the student to earn a degree in four years.

Credit for Life Experience: Yes, first speak with the Coordinator of Nontraditional Study at Heidelberg. Heidelberg is a member of the East Central College Consortium, a coalition of "seven private, liberal arts schools" which "assesses the college-level knowledge that people have acquired outside the traditional classroom." This consortium comprises the following:

Executive Director
East Central College Consortium
Mount Union College
Alliance, Ohio

(216) 821-5320

Coordinator
Nontraditional Study
Bethany College
Bethany, West Virginia 26032

(304) 829-7000

Dean—Weekend College
Hiram College
Hiram, Ohio 44234

(216) 569-3211

Coordinator
Nontraditional Study
Marietta College
Marietta, Ohio 45750

(614) 373-4643

Coordinator
Nontraditional Study
Mount Union College
Alliance, Ohio 44601

(216) 821-5320

Coordinator
Nontraditional Study
Muskingum College
New Concord, Ohio 43762

(614) 826-8211

Coordinator
Nontraditional Study
Westminster College
New Wilmington, Pennsylvania 16142

(412) 946-8761

Tuition: Twelve to 16 semester hours was $2445 for 1980–81, or $140 per semester hour.

Time Required: At least one year, but probably a good deal longer.

Oklahoma

Independent and Correspondence Study
Oklahoma State University
001 Classroom Building
Stillwater, Oklahoma 74078

(405) 624-6390

Independent Study Department
The University of Oklahoma
Continuing Education and Public Service
1700 ASP Avenue, Room B-1
Norman, Oklahoma 73037

(405) 325-1921
(800) 942-5702 (in Oklahoma only)

Background: State-operated independent and correspondence program. Accredited by the North Central Association of Colleges and Schools and a member of the National University of Continuing Education Association.

Admission: Open to anyone 21 years of age or older. You need not be admitted to the university to enroll. If you intend to use this credit for a degree at Oklahoma, or at another school, you must secure permission.

Degrees Offered: No fully external degrees are offered. You may use up to 30 semester hours earned via correspondence toward a degree.

Tuition: $35 per semester hour. Out-of-state students are charged a $10 administration fee. High school tuition is $35 per one half unit, which equals one semester.

Study Program: Routine correspondence study, but a good selection of courses are available. Mid-term and final examinations are required.

Credit for Life Experience: Only through CLEP, ACT-PEP and advanced standing or challenge examinations.

Time Required: One year is allowed to complete a course, and a six-month extension may be had for an additional $5 per credit hour fee. No course may be completed in less than 30 days.

Oregon

**Marylhurst College for
Lifelong Learning**
Marylhurst, Oregon 97036

(503) 636-8141
(503) 224-5828

Background: A program designed for adults. Average age of student body is 38. Marylhurst was founded in 1893 as St. Mary's College, then a women's college. Because of declining enrollments, Marylhurst was established as an independent coeducational institution in 1974 to serve adults.

Degrees Awarded: Bachelor of Arts (in Art, Crafts, Communication, Humanities, Science/Math, Pastoral Ministries and Interdisciplinary Studies): Bachelor of Science in Management; Bachelor of Arts or Bachelor of Music in Music.

Admission: High school diploma or equivalent.

Requirements: A total of 180 quarter hours, which includes 60 upper-division credits and 40 credits through Marylhurst.

Study Program: Credits are earned through resident courses, independent studies, internships, examinations, and some correspondence courses.

Tuition: A fee of $85 per quarter.

Credit for Experiential Learning: Under the Prior Learning Experience program, a student may earn up to 90 quarter-hour credits through portfolio preparation. Internships, travel study, credit by examination and course waivers also afford credit for prior learning.

Time Required: You can expect a minimum of two semesters.

Off Campus Degree Program
Linfield College
McMinnville, Oregon 97128-9989

(503) 472-4121, ext. 269
800-452-4176 (toll free in Oregon)

Background: A traditional school with a strong nontraditional program, and satellite programs operating throughout Oregon.

Admission: Open.

Degrees Awarded: B.S. in management; B.A. in Liberal Studies; B.S. in Nursing.

Tuition: $75 per credit hour.

Credit for Life Experience: Yes, "up to 95 semester hours can be earned through portfolio assessment or a combination of portfolio assessment, CLEP, and credit by examination." The Linfield College portfolio assessment fee is also rather reasonable. A student might opt for their portfolio assessment program and then transfer the credits to another institution. You should always check to verify that credits may be easily transferred.

CREDIT HOURS	BASIC COST	ADDITIONAL COST PER SEMESTER HOURS (S.H.)
Under 25 S.H.	$ 75	$15 per S.H.
25-50 S.H.	$125	$15 per S.H.
51-75 S.H.	$175	$15 per S.H.
Over 75 S.H.	$225	$15 per S.H.

Time Required: A minimum of 30 semester hours with Linfield is required for a degree. At least 15 hours in your major must be taken with Linfield to earn their degree.

Pennsylvania

Dean of Continuing Education
Neumann College
Aston, Pennsylvania 19014

(215) 459-0905

Background: This program was established in September 1974. It consists of a variety of approaches, including seminars and independent study. One hundred and twenty semester hours with a minimum GPA of 2.0 are required for graduation.

Admission: Persons 21 or older.

Degrees Awarded: B.S.; B.A.

Tuition: Not available.

Study Program: In addition to customary three-credit courses, the "AIM Program includes six-credit seminars, independent study, assessment of degree-related life-experience learning, and the opportunity to design an individualized degree program according to life and career goals." Contact with the campus is required and classes are held in the evening. Sixty semester hours of this degree must be in liberal arts courses. Up to 30 semester hours may be taken through independent study.

Credit for Life Experience: Yes, up to sixty semester hours may be earned through: (1) portfolio assessment, (2) challenge examinations, (3) CLEP, (4) award of credit for recognized non-credit courses and programs and/or professional registry. Evening courses meet one evening each week for 15 weeks.

Time Required: At least two semesters.

Adult External Degree Program
Elizabethtown College
Elizabethtown, Pennsylvania 17022

(717) 367-1151

Background: Elizabethtown College was founded in 1899 and is fully accredited by the Middle States Association of Colleges and Secondary Schools. The Adult External Degree Program was established in 1972.

Degrees Awarded: The Associate of Arts, Associate of Science, Bachelor of Liberal Studies, Bachelor of Professional Studies.

Admission: The applicant must have a minimum of 26 credit hours to be accepted into the associate degree program, 50 credit hours for the bachelor's program. Also, there are three all-day Saturday sessions at the college, for which seminar the student earns three credit hours if working on an A.A. or 4 hours for a B.A.

Requirements: In addition to the requirements set forth above, the student will complete a Degree Project, which is an "in-depth" study of an aspect of his or her major. The student is also awarded credit for courses successfully completed with a C or better at accredited colleges or universities. Elizabethtown College also awards credit for the College Level Examination Program. According to their literature: "Six semester hours of credit are awarded for a score in the 40th percentile or above on each of the general examinations and three to six hours of credit are awarded on subject examinations on which the applicant has achieved a score in the 50th percentile or above."

Tuition: The cost of this program will vary widely, depending upon the student's background, and how many credits he or she will have to complete at a local institution. Tuition for Elizabethtown College is $1800 for the B.A., $1200 for the A.A.

Credit for Life Experience: Yes, Elizabethtown is very progressive in this aspect of nontraditional education and awards the appropriate college credit for "learning achieved in employment, community and avocational experience, as well as through disciplined reading and observation."

Time Required: The college's brochure does not state any minimum period of time to earn a degree but a well-motivated student should be able to advance rapidly.

The Lifelong Learning Program
Westminster College
New Wilmington, Pennsylvania 16142

(412) 946-8761

Background: Westminster is a member of the East Central College Consortium (see others in the entry on **Heidelberg College,** Ohio). This is not an external-degree program. "For those who live within a reasonable commuting distance of the college, we offer an innovative, flexible, college-credit program open to individuals seeking coursework for personal or professional development. . . ."

Admission: High school diploma or equivalent.

Degrees Awarded: B.A.; B.S.; Bachelor of Music.

Tuition: A fee of $485 for each 3.5 semester hours.

Study Program: Regular classroom work is scheduled evenings and Saturdays.

Credit for Life Experience: Yes, up to two years of credit but only to Westminster degree candidates. A $395 fee for assessment.

Time Required: At least two semesters.

Office of Continuing Education
Cabrini College
Eagle and King of Prussia Roads
Radnor, Pennsylvania 19087

(215) 687-2100

Background: Founded in 1957 by the Missionary Sisters of the Sacred Heart, Cabrini is a liberal arts college. There are 600 full-time students and 250 part-time people in the continuing-education program. Senior citizens may enroll in courses on a space-available basis for a fee of $5.00. Contact with the campus is required even though there is a limited amount of External Study.

Admission: High school diploma, and/or transcripts of one's educational background.

Tuition: Full-time tuition is $3850, or $118 per semester hour. Evening tuiton is $88 per semester hour.

Degrees Awarded: B.A.; B.S.; Bachelor of Science in Education; Master of Education.

Study Program: Weekend, evening course work.

Credit for Life Experience: Yes, through portfolio assessment and through credit for noncollegiate training based upon the recommendations of the American Council on Education's National Guide to Credit Recommendations for Noncollegiate Courses.

Time Required: At least one year and probably longer.

Open Learning
Pennsylvania State University
128 Mitchell Building
University Park, Pennsylvania 16802

(800) 252-3592 (Pennsylvania residents)
(800) 458-3617 (out of state)

Background: Penn State first developed correspondence instruction at the turn of the century and has been an innovative institution since that time. Penn State pioneered radio, film, and television correspondence courses. About 170 credit courses and 85 noncredit courses are offered. If you live in Pennsylvania, a number of courses are available through "PENNARAMA," which transmits courses via cable television systems. Cable television is unquestionably the future mode for adult education, as the United States is wired nearly everywhere for such transmissions. High school correspondence courses are available for residents and nonresidents. Individuals 60 and over may enroll for credit courses at half tuition. Exams are required, and proctors may be arranged for out-of-state students.

Admission: High school diploma.

Degrees Awarded: Associate degree in Letters, Arts and Sciences. No external Bachelors.

Tuition: A fee of $46 per credit hour.

Study Program: The method employed here uses textbooks, study guides, written lessons, tape recordings, and the feedback from instructors.

Credit for Life Experience: No.

Time Required: One year is allowed to complete a course, but may request two six-month time extensions.

South Carolina

Correspondence Study
University of South Carolina
915 Gregg Street
Columbia, South Carolina 29208

(803) 777-2188

Background: Initially chartered in 1801 and reorganized several times, the university's institutional objective is to "furnish both liberal and professional education to the people of South Carolina." Although there is no external degree or credit for experiential learning, this program has a significant number of courses that can aid a student in earning a degree elsewhere. There is no graduate credit available from this program. Courses from this program may be used for Teacher Certification purposes. "Telecourses" are also available in South Carolina.

Admission: Open entry. The student need not be formally admitted to the University of South Carolina. The prospective student should insure that he or she is eligible for admission, in case you decide to pursue a degree with the university.

Degrees Awarded: No external degree is available at this time. However, "a total of thirty semester hours earned through correspondence study may be applied towards a degree to be granted by the University. . . ." You would need the dean of your college to accomplish this task. Also, thirty semester hours must be earned as a resident student before earning a degree.

Tuition: A fee of $25 per semester hour.

Courses Available: Business—28 (including accounting, business law and management); Economics—9; Education—6; English—19; History—18; Mathematics and Statistics—7; Psychology—11. A number of other courses are also available.

Time Required: A maximum of three courses may be taken at one time. No course may be completed in less than two months. One year is the limit for completing a course. You may have a three-month extension to complete a course.

South Dakota

State-Wide Educational Services
Center for Continuing Education
University of South Dakota
Vermillion, South Dakota 57069

(605) 677-5011

Background: The University of South Dakota has been offering correspondence courses since 1915–16. There is a limit of 30 semester hours of correspondence work for a baccalaureate degree with this university. No graduate credit is offered via correspondence.

Admission: Open-entry, open-exit. Admission to correspondence study does not constitute admission to the university.

Tuition: $31 per semester hour, plus textbooks.

Degrees Awarded: None through this program.

Study Program: "Generally, there are eight assignments, in a one-hour course, sixteen in a two-hour course, twenty-four in a three-hour course and thirty-two in a four-hour course." A few courses have midterm exams and all courses have a final.

Credit for Life Experience: No.

Time Required: One year is allowed to complete a course. A six-month extension may be obtained and a fee of $10 is charged. Two correspondence courses is the maximum a student may take.

Tennessee

Director of Admissions, or
Assistant Academic Dean for Nontraditional Studies
Lincoln Memorial University
Harrogate, Tennessee 37752

(615) 869-3611

Background: Founded in the late 1800s, this is a private liberal arts, nonsectarian college located in the heart of Appalachia. Lincoln also operates a home-study program. The grade of F—failing—is not recorded on the student's official transcript. Lincoln is on the quarter system.

Admission: Requirements appear to be very flexible and seek to give everyone the opportunity for a college education. You must be at least 21 years of age to enter the Home Study Program and have successfully completed at least two years of postsecondary education.

Tuition: A fee of $45 per credit hour for part-time students; $2025 for full-time students who commute.

Degrees Awarded: Associate and baccalaureate. A Bachelor of Professional Studies may be earned through the Home Study Program, with a concentration in Business Administration or Applied Science.

Study Program: Home study, directed and independent study, as well as routine class work. The last three quarters or 45 quarter hours must be earned "in residence."
   The Home Study Program has been in development over the past few years: "Using specially created modular materials, the learning experiences provided are designed to develop skills, concepts and learning activities which are equivalent to those encountered through the on-campus program."

Credit for Life Experience: Yes. The cost is $10 per hour for each quarter-hour credit awarded. They will accept up to two years through CLEP.

Time Required: This will depend solely upon the student.

Center for Extended Learning
Division of Continuing Education
The University of Tennessee
420 Communications & Extension Building
Knoxville, Tennessee 37916

(615) 974-5135

Background: The Department of Correspondence Study began at this institution in 1923. Students at the university may take up to one-quarter of their courses through independent/correspondence study.

Admission: Open-entry, open-exit. Admission to correspondence study does not constitute admission to the university.

Tuition:

2 quarter hours $50	1 semester hour $37.00
3 quarter hours $75	2 semester hours $74.00
4 quarter hours $100	3 semester hours $111.00

Degrees Awarded: None.

Study Program: Standard correspondence study, which may include audio-visual media in some circumstances. A final examination is required.

Credit for Life Experience: No.

Time Required: One year from the official date of enrollment. One extension of six months can be obtained at a cost of $10.

Texas

East Texas State University
Commerce, Texas 75428

(214) 886-5922

Background: A correspondence continuing-education program for high school graduates and college students seeking to supplement their education. Those seeking to utilize these credits for a degree must procure permission from the Dean of their college.

Degrees Awarded: None.

Admission: Open to all. If students seek credit toward graduation, they must meet the same criteria as resident students.

Requirements: Not available.

Study Program: One course at a time is recommended, but the student may take two. No course may be completed in less than 45 days, and each course must be completed within one year. Six-month extensions may be obtained. There are midterm and final examinations. To take exams students must make arrangements that are satisfactory to ETSU.

Tuition: $25 per semester hour.

Time Required: See Study Program.

Utah

Department of Independent Study
Brigham Young University
210 HRCB
Provo, Utah 84602

(801) 378-2868

Background: Although this is not a likely quick-degree program, the Bachelor of Independent Studies Degree offered by Brigham Young University is quite impressive. Furthermore, the excellent reputation of the Mormon religion, in general, will lend legitimacy to the degree. You are expected to "maintain the ideals and standards of the Church of Jesus Christ of Latter-Day Saints" while in this program.

   According to a Brigham Young brochure, a number of seminars are required to earn this degree. You may avoid some of these seminars providing you transfer into this program with enough credit hours. Even so, it seems likely that some campus contact will be required.

Admission: In addition to the customary procedures, you must also: "(A) submit Code of Honor properly executed; (B) submit confidential report from applicant's bishop, pastor, or church administrator; (C) take any tests, if recommended by evaluation committee."

Degrees Offered: Among other degrees, Brigham Young's independent-studies program offers an Associate of Arts in Genealogy. "There are two study options available for you to choose from. The *professional* research option is for those who want to pass a national accreditation examination and/or do genealogical research for hire. The *personal* research option will help a person become competent in researching personal and family lines." Other degrees are offered in Justice Administration, Home and Family Development, and English.

Tuition: Tuition will vary according to how much college and experiential credit are transferred into the program. A minimum of $1500.

Study Program: Routine correspondence study.

Credit for Life Experience: No.

Time Required: According to Brigham Young's brochure, "The Bachelor's degree normally takes from three to six years to complete, as most adults will be studying on a part-time basis. Those devoting more time to the program or receiving waivers may complete the degree in less time."

Division of Adult Programs
Westminster College
1840 South 1300 East
Salt Lake City, Utah 84105

(801) 484-7651

Background: Founded in 1875 as a Presbyterian Preparatory School, Westminster has evolved into a fully accedited private college. Contact with the campus is required. 124 semester hours are required for graduation. Westminster also offers a Legal Assistant Training Program for $1800, which requires 30 semester units of course work.

Admission: A GPA of 2.0 or higher and a high school diploma.

Degrees Awarded: B.A., B.S.

Tuition: $79.50 per semester hour for the student's first three semesters.

Study Program: Evening and weekend classes are offered on the campus and at several business locations.

Credit for Life Experience: Yes, as many as 45 semester hours may be earned from work experience, volunteer service, in-service training, personal study, etc. The student must prepare a portfolio for evaluation. It is necessary to attend a portfolio workshop, which costs $106 tuition and earns one semester hour.

Time Required: At least 30 semester hours must be earned at Westminster, since a maximum of 94 hours may be transferred in or earned through experiential credit.

Vermont

**The School for
International Training**
Brattleboro, Vermont 05301

(802) 257-7751
(800) 451-4465

Background: The School for International Training (SIT) was founded in 1964 by the Experiment in International Living (EIL), a private, nonprofit organization established in 1932. EIL is the "oldest international exchange organization in the country." This international and intercultural education provides professional programs to those seeking careers in international affairs. The SIT offers "highly individualized programs" combining "traditional and nontraditional work in the classroom, work on an internship, and work in the community . . . ." The goal of this experience-based program is the development of problem-solving skills.

These degrees, with the exception of an external Master's Program in Intercultural Management, require campus contact. SIT is "unique in that the majority of its students on campus are from foreign countries. We feel that this is a great advantage not offered by other educational institutions. We are proud of the opportunity this affords students for daily interaction with others from a variety of educational and cultural backgrounds. We consider this to be an important cross-cultural experience. Thus, on-campus residence is an intrinsic part of the program and students are encouraged to live on campus.

Accredited by the New England Association of Schools and Colleges.

Degrees Awarded: Bachelor's Degree in International Studies (World Issues Program); Master of Arts in Teaching Second Languages; Master's Program in Intercultural

Management. The external Master's Program in Intercultural Management is for people "unable to complete the three phase course within its on-campus period." This "enables qualified working professionals to earn their Master's degree over an extended period of time." The program is of "special interest to professionals in social service agencies, foreign studies and student affairs, advising, and international business and law."

Admission: Requirements vary according to the program selected. The B.A. program is four semesters in length and open to those with 60 credit hours. The Master of Arts in Teaching Second Languages requires a bachelor's degree and language proficiency. The Master's Program in Intercultural Management requires a bachelor's degree and fluency in another language. An interview is required of all applicants to these programs.

Study Program: Semesters on campus are followed by semesters off campus. There is an ongoing process of evaluation throughout all of these programs.

Tuition: The costs of these programs vary from about $6500 to $9000.

Time Required: About two years for all options.

Office of External Programs
Vermont State Colleges
P.O. Box #292
Montpelier, Vermont 05602

(802) 828-2401

Background: A variety of external-type degree and study programs are available through the five members of the Vermont State system. Johnson State has an external degree and is "statewide, learner-centered and competency based." A minimum of 60 semester hours are required for admission and it "culminates in either a B.A. or B.S. degree in 8 or 10 pre-specified areas." Contact:

> Ms. Joanna Noel
> Director of the External Degree Program
> Johnson State College
> Johnson, Vermont 05656

This program is for "off-campus individualized instruction" to adults.

Admission: A total of 60 semester hours for the external degree. You must also show that you are capable of doing the work involved.

Degrees Awarded: B.A.; B.S.

Tuition: About $1500 for in-state students, full time; $3100 for full-time out-of-state students. Students from the New England region pay in-state tuition plus a 25 percent premium.

Study Program: The external program at Johnson State is "organized through learning contracts."

Credit for Life Experience: Yes, the Assessment of Prior Learning Program is a "multi-institutional program that assesses the prior, experiential learning of adult students."

Time Required: No less than one year.

Goddard Graduate Program
Vermont College of
Norwich University
Plainfield, Vermont 05667

(802) 454-8311

Background: Strongly nontraditional program located in Vermont, Goddard's program was absorbed into Vermont College in 1981. This program serves people "from 17 to 70" through individual study. Accredited by the New England Association of Schools and Colleges, Goddard offers residential and low-residential modes of study. Young people entering from high school normally enter the residential mode of education. Each term at Goddard begins with a nine-day "All College Meeting," and intensive planning period. There are three fourteen-week terms. Residential students spend two terms at Goddard and one term in "work, travel, social action, reflection, or relaxation." The low-residence student spends all three terms studying. Individual study plans revolve around a core or "cluster group" of students with the same basic interest. Goddard is located close to Plainfield, in rural Vermont, about ten miles from the state capital of Montpelier.

Degrees Awarded: Bachelor of Arts, Master of Arts, or the Master of Fine Arts in writing.

Admission: "The basic criterion for admission to Goddard is being ready, willing, and able to participate fully in the demanding Goddard program." High school and college transcripts, if any, tell a certain amount about the student. More important are the personal statements "in which the applicant writes about his or her educational experiences and aims in a social and personal context," plus the personal interview with a Goddard counselor and one or more faculty members.

Study Program: "Studies are based in questions, tasks, or problems and often draw on ideas and resources from many academic disciplines. They usually involve inquiry, information gathering, action, and evaluation as ways of developing and testing ideas, opinions, and abilities." Low-residence students are to draw upon the cultural resources of their communities, to literally use the world as their classroom.

Requirements: The student must satisfactorily complete course and field work, as well as a major independent study.

Credit for Life Experience: The 1978-79 catalog states that "up to two semesters of advancement towards the Bachelor of Arts degree to students who can demonstrate and document learning through such experiences" is granted. You may not make such an application until having been admitted. High College Level Placement Examination scores can earn advanced placement for the student entering Goddard with fewer than thirty college credits.

Tuition: A fee of $8700 for the two-term academic year for residential students, which covers tuition, room, board, and the three All College Meetings. A fee of $3600 for low-residence students for the three-term year, due in three equal installments. Financial aid is available and generally consists of loans and grants.

Time Required: A minimum of four semesters is required regardless of how much credit the student transfers in.

Virginia

Mary Baldwin College
Staunton, Viginia 24401

(703) 885-0811

Background: Founded in 1842 under the aegis of the Presbyterian Church of the United States as a woman's school, Mary Baldwin College is a four-year liberal arts school located in the beautiful Shenandoah Valley of Virginia. The Adult Degree Program is a "nonresidential, individualized Bachelor of Arts degree program designed primarily to meet the educational needs of mature adults."

Admission: The criteria for admission vary slightly depending upon whether one is a freshman, advanced student or part-time student. The standards of this school are high, and freshmen should be in the upper-quarter of their high school class. Admission to the Adult Degree Program is open to men and women who are 21 or older.

Tuition: Costs will vary according to the student's program. Annual tuition is $1025. Directed independent-study tutorials are $190; non-directed independent-study tutorials are $110. Daytime coursework at Mary Baldwin is $261 per course. Prior learning evaluation is a minimum of $50, and will vary according to the portfolio.

Degrees Awarded: B.A.

Study Program: Learning contracts are established that state what is to be studied, and how the learning experience is to be evaluated. This may include study at other colleges, independent study with the faculty, approved off-campus tutors, and special projects.

Credit for Life Experience: Yes.

Time Required: A minimum of 36 course units from Mary Baldwin. One may be able to transfer a certain number of credits in with permission.

Washington

Office of Alternative Learning Experiences
Whatcom Community College
5217 Northwest Road
Bellingham, Washington 98226

(206) 676-2170
(206) 384-1541

Background: This community college was established in 1967, and is accredited by the Northwest Association of Schools and Colleges. It exists to serve people in the surrounding community. Contract learning, Individualized Instruction, Cooperative Work Experience, Credit by Examination, Challenge Examinations and CLEP are available. Whatcom is on the quarter-hour credit system.

Admission: High school diploma or GED.

Tuition: A fee of $457.50 for full-time residents; $1816.50 for full-time nonresidents.

Degrees Awarded: None is available through an external or correspondence-degree program.

Study Program: Routine class work, except for the special programs that allow for the establishment of credit, as set forth above.

Credit for Life Experience: "A student may earn up to 15 credits through military experience." Such credit may only be used for the A.A. and A.S. degrees.

Time Required: This will depend upon the student but one-year minimum is quite likely.

Office of Independent Study
University of Washington
222 Lewis Hall, DW—30
Seattle, Washington 98195

(206) 543-2350

Office of Independent Study
Western Washington University
Center for Continuing Education
Bellingham, Washington 98225

(206) 676-3320

Continuing University Studies
Courses by Correspondence
Washington State University
Van Doren 208
Pullman, Washington 99164

(509) 335-3557

State Board for Community College Education
319 East Seventh Avenue
WEA Building
Olympia, Washington 98504

(This last address is for information about nontraditonal programs at the community-college level.)

Background: The correspondence booklet available from this school lists over "140 courses from 8 of the schools and colleges at the University of Washington." The other two campuses included here have different correspondence offerings. All of these programs cooperate with the Defense Activity for Non-traditional Education Support.

The ELDERHOSTEL program is available at the Pullman campus. This is a "Nationwide educational program for persons 60 years of age or older." The ELDERHOSTEL offers several one-week sessions each summer and fall. "Housing, meals, noncredit classes, and a number of extracurricular events are included in each week's program."

Admission: Open-entry, open-exit for those with a high school diploma or who are over 18 years of age. Admission to correspondence study does not constitute admission to the university.

132

Tuition: A fee of $26 per credit hour at the University of Washington—Seattle. Tuition is $25 per credit hour at Western Washington University. Tuition is $33 per semester hour at the Pullman campus.

Degrees Awarded: It is not possible to earn a degree at the University of Washington exclusively through correspondence study. However, a significant number of credits toward a degree may be earned through correspondence study.

Study Program: Routine correspondence study. Final examinations are required. Individually Designed Supervised study is available to those who have a UW professor willing to supervise it, providing it is a part of the undergraduate curriculum. No graduate credit is available through independent study.

Western Washington University is on the quarter-hour system (three quarters equals two semester hours). A maximum of 45 quarter hours may be applied to the bachelor's degree at this institution. The selection of correspondence courses is considerably better at the Seattle campus.

Credit for Life Experience: Not at this particular institution although it is available from Eastern Washington University and other members of the University of Washington system.

Credit for life experience is available through:

Eastern Washington University
Center for Extended Learning
Credit Through Evaluation Program
Cheney, Washington 99004

(509) 359-2402
(509) 458-6221

Time Required: No less than two months to complete a course, and no more than one year.

Washington, D.C.

Correspondence Study Programs
Graduate School
United States Department of Agriculture
Room 6847, South Building
14th and Independence Avenues, S.W.
Washington, D.C. 20250

(202) 447-7123

Background: Founded in 1921, this "institution" has a dual mission: to help enrich lives and improve job performance, and to increase organizational efficiency. the Graduate School *does not* grant degrees and has never sought the authority to do so. The Graduate School offers standard courses, and you should check first with any institution you are considering transferring these credits to; not accredited. The faculty is recruited from "scholars and officials" in the Washington, D.C., community. Correspondence study; some classes are offered in Washington, D.C. This is a handy program for government people, as well as those abroad, and may have some offerings not available elsewhere.

Degrees Awarded: None.

Admissions: Open-entry at any time regardless of employment or residence. Full payment for a course must accompany the registration form. Fees vary according to the course taken.

Requirements/Study Program: Self-paced correspondence study in Administration, Communications (i.e., English), Financial Management and Accounting, Library Technology, Mathematics and Statistics, Personnel Administration, Sciences and Engineering. The number of lessons and credits per course varies according to the subject matter. For example, Hydrology II is 15 lessons for 4.5 credits, at a cost of $139; Basic Indexing is 13 lessons, for 3 credits, at a cost of $110.

Southeastern University
501 Eye Street, S.W.
Washington, D.C. 20024

(202) 488-8162

Background: This is a nonprofit, independent institution chartered by Congress whose origins go back to 1879, when programs were first offered by the Washington Young Men's Christian Association. This is a career-oriented school that has a significant number of adult students attending full or part-time. Southeastern University of Washington, D.C., is not affiliated with any other schools. It is accredited by a variety of organizations. Southeastern is a Servicemember Opportunity College, which allows members of the military to "pursue educational programs through a variety of traditional and non-traditional means on campuses and military institutions in a variety of instructional modes and at times appropriate to their duty assignments."

Admission: High school diploma or equivalent plus "a satisfactory SAT score," for undergraduates. Students from abroad must score at least 550 on the Test of English as a Foreign Language (TOEFL). Applicants for graduate-degree programs must have a bachelor's degree, and a 3.0 grade-point average, plus a satisfactory score on the graduate admissions test.

Tuition: A fee of $80 per hour for undergraduates; $100 per hour for graduate students. A variety of financial aid is available for the student who can show need.

Degrees Awarded: Bachelor's and master's degrees are offered in a wide variety of business-related specialties too numerous to be listed here.

Credit for Life Experience: Yes, the student submits "a detailed description of the life/work experience to be evaluated" and specifies to which Southeastern courses that life experience applies. Programs such as CLEP, DANTES, Credit by Examination, and credit for military experience and training also exist.

Time Required: This will depend on the student and the background that he or she brings to the school, but at least a year is likely.

Trinity College
Franklin Street and Michigan Avenue, NE
Washington, D.C. 20017

(202) 269-2201

Background: Founded in 1897, Trinity is the oldest Catholic women's college initially founded as such. Trinity offers a degree-completion program and the Sustained Trinity Education Program. STEP allows a woman to take up to 11 credits per semester without necessarily working toward a degree.

Admission: Credits from other colleges may be transferred to Trinity. The equivalency of course offerings is determined by the Coordinator of Student Records.

Degrees Awarded: Bachelor, Master of Arts in Teaching and the Master of Arts.

Tuition: A fee of $4,700 for day students; $147 per credit hour for part-time students. If you have been out of college for more than five years a reduced rate of $100 per credit will apply to the first six taken at Trinity. A fee of $100 per credit for an audit course.

Credit for Experiential Learning: After completing nine credits at Trinity, you can apply for experiential credit. A maximum of 16 experiential credits may be earned. The Director of Continuing Education and the Chair of the Department determine eligibility. These 16 credits are in addition to the 32 credits you must earn at Trinity for a degree.

Time Required: No fewer than two semesters and probably a good deal more. This program should be of special interest to those in Maryland, Washington, D.C., and Virginia.

Wisconsin

Continuing Education Program
Office of Admissions
Beloit College
Beloit, Wisconsin 53511

(608) 365-3391

Background: Independent, nonsectarian, chartered in 1846, and "widely known for its approach to undergraduate education, Beloit College was among the first to successfully introduce a year-round, three-term academic program that emphasizes individual learning over institutional instruction." Contact with the campus is required.

Admission: Students must be at least 25 years of age and may not have been registered at Beloit within two years of admission to this program. Regular admission standards are applied to those seeking admission.

Tuition: A fee of $275 per full-unit course, one-fourth of the current tuition.

Degrees Awarded: B.A.; B.S.; Master of Teaching.

Study Program: Routine study, as supplemented by credit by examination.

Credit for Life Experience: Not as such, but credit is available by examination.

Time Required: A residency requirement of two terms of full-time on-campus study must be met.

University of Wisconsin—Extension
Independent Study
432 North Lake Street
Madison, Wisconsin 53706

(608) 263-2055

Background: Independent study has been offered by the University of Wisconsin since 1906. Of special interest here is a brief note in their catalog that states: "Correspondence courses may be of special interest in connection with some of the new nontraditional degree programs now being established, such as the New York Regents' Degree for which there is no residency requirement." High school and Continuing Education Units are also available.

Admission: Open-entry, open-exit. Admission to correspondence study does not constitute admission to the University of Wisconsin. This program offers over 400 correspondence courses that should be of considerable utility to those earning an external degree elsewhere.

Tuition: Varies according to the course but is comparable with other correspondence institutions.

Degrees Awarded: None through independent study for individuals who do not live in Wisconsin. There are four Extended Degree Programs available for residents of Wisconsin, each with different requirements: (1) The Bachelor of Science—Business Administration Degree (offered by UW—Platteville); (2) The Bachelor of Arts—General Studies Degree (UW—Green Bay); (3) The Individually Designed Major (UW—Superior); (4) The Bachelor of Science—Broad Area Studies in Agriculture (UW—River Falls College of Agriculture). The catalog also states: "You may earn up to the residency requirement toward a bachelor's degree from any degree-granting institution in the University of Wisconsin system through Independent Study. We urge you to check with a resident adviser or an extension adviser to be sure the course you choose is appropriate to your degree objective. Credits earned in Independent Study will transfer to other units of the University of Wisconsin System *but not grades or grade points*" (emphasis added).

Extended Degree Program Advisor
The Bachelor of Science—Business Administration Degree
University of Wisconsin—Platteville
510 Pioneer Tower
Platteville, Wisconsin 53818

(608) 342-1468

Extended Degree Program
The Bachelor of Arts—General Studies Degree
University of Wisconsin—Green Bay
Green Bay, Wisconsin 54302

(414) 465-2423

Extended Degree Program Advisor
The Individually Designed Major
University of Wisconsin—Superior
237 Old Main
Superior, Wisconsin 54880

(715) 392-9271

Extended Degree Program
The Bachelor of Science—Broad Area Studies in Agriculture
College of Agriculture
University of Wisconsin—River Falls
River Falls, Wisconsin 54022

(715) 425-3239

Study Program: Routine correspondence study involving a syllabus, textbooks, occasionally audio-visual media, written assignments, and a final examination.

Credit for Life Experience: No.

Time Required: One year is allowed to complete a correspondence course.

Cardinal Stritch College
6801 Yates Road
Milwaukee, Wisconsin 53217

(414) 352-5400

Background: Founded in 1937. A small Catholic, independent, coed liberal arts college sponsored by the Sisters of St. Francis Assisi. It "recognizes that adult learners have unique needs and specific interests." Student body 111—1200. Although they understand the problems of the adult student, contact with the campus is required to earn this degree.

Admisson: High school diploma or its equivalent.

Degrees Awarded: A.A.; B.A. in over 20 academic majors; B.S. in Home Economics; B.S. in Professional Arts for Registered Nurses; M.A. in reading and special education; Masters of Education/Professional Development in Teaching degree.

Tuition: A fee of $1800 full-time; $115 per semester hour.

Credit for Life Experience: Yes. Also credit by examination. Up to 60 credit hours may be earned by examination of the bachelor's degree; 30 for the A.A.

Time Required: At least two semesters, and probably more.

Director of Admissions
University of Wisconsin—Platteville
725 West Main Street
Platteville, Wisconsin 53818

(608) 342-1125

Extended Degree Program Counselor
University of Wisconsin—Platteville
511 Pioneer Tower
Platteville, Wisconsin 53818

(608) 342-1467

Background: The Department of Business Administration offers a B.S. through the Extended Degree Program. "This enables adults with partially completed baccalaureate degrees to finish them without attendance on campus." This campus does not offer correspondence courses although the University of Wisconsin system does.

Admission: Open-entry to qualified students, open-exit.

Degrees Awarded: B.S.

Tuition: A fee of $40 per semester hour for residents of Wisconsin; $129 for nonresidents; full-time tuition is $488 for residents and $1562 for nonresidents.

Study Program: Independent-study courses, radio and television, program-learning sources, internships, among other methods, are used.

Credit for Life Experience: Yes.

Time Required: At least two semesters.

Wyoming

School of Extended Studies and Public Service
Correspondence Study Department
University of Wyoming
Box #3294, University Station
Laramie, Wyoming 82071

(307) 766-6322

Background: Correspondence instruction has been offered since 1893. About 130 college and 40 high school courses are available. Up to 24 semester hours toward the bachelor's degree at the University of Wyoming may be correspondence study. No graduate credit is available.

Admission: Open-entry, but this does not constitute admission to the University.

Tuition: A fee of $21 per semester hour.

Degrees Awarded: None through this program.

Study Program: Routine correspondence study.

Credit for Life Experience: No.

Time Required: One year. An extension of one year may be requested.

7

BIBLE COLLEGES, LAW SCHOOLS, AND MEDICAL SCHOOLS

There are three types of schools that have not been fully explored within this book: Bible colleges, law schools, and medical schools. Within this chapter a small amount of information will be provided for those who may be interested in pursuing a course of study in one of these areas.

Bible Colleges

There is a large number of Bible schools of all types and religions around the United States and Canada. This fact and the wide diversity of these Bible schools make it almost impossible to evaluate each program appropriately.

The Bible-college movement dates back at least a century when they were assigned the function of preparing individuals for church-related vocations. Education at a Bible college consists of general education, professional courses, and biblical studies. General education courses are similar to those at any college or university. Some Bible colleges do not teach any particular religious precepts, while others may adhere strictly to Fundamentalist, Protestant, or some other viewpoint.

A letter from the American Association of Bible Colleges in June 1982 flatly states: "We do not consider our institutions to be 'nontraditional.' However, a number of our institutions provide various forms of adult education." Nontraditional or not, the fact remains that many of these institutions are involved in some or all of the following modes of instruction: self-paced instruction and/or correspondence credit, credit for experiential learning, intensive seminars, individualized learning contracts, etc.

There are different approaches to religious education, a major complicating factor in assessing which of these institutions has educationally solid programs. Because of this and because of the sheer numbers of such institutions, it is recommended that those interested in pursuing such an education contact the following organizations:

American Association of Bible Colleges
P.O. Box #1523
Fayetteville, Arkansas 72701

(501) 521-8164

The American Association of Bible Colleges is recognized by the U.S. Office of Education as a national professional accrediting agency. Another organization which can supply you with information and the addresses of schools is the:

Association for Clinical Pastoral Education, Inc.
Interchurch Center, Suite #450
475 Riverside Drive
New York, New York 10115

(212) 870-2558

A final piece of advice worth remembering is this: Shop around very carefully for a Bible school, and triple-check to insure that any credential you obtain fulfills its function for you. Some Bible schools appears to be one-man operations out to profit from the unsuspecting. Others have curricula that are so intellectually lightweight that absolutely no one will accept their degrees as a valid credential. You must also always check with individual state Department of Education concerned to insure that any given Bible school is licensed and authorized to grant valid credentials.

Here is a list of such schools to contact for further information:

AMERICAN ASSOCIATION OF BIBLE COLLEGES

Member Schools Offering Correspondence Courses

Appalachian Bible College
Bradley, West Virginia 25818

Berkshire Christian College
200 Stockbridge Road
Lennox, MA 01240

Central Baptist College
CBC Station
Conway, AR 72032

Central Bible College
3000 N. Grant St.
Springfield, MO 65802

Cincinnati Bible College
2700 Glenway Avenue
Cincinnati, OH 45204

Dallas Bible College
8733 La Prada Dr.
Dallas, TX 75228

Emmanuel College of Chr. Min.
Box 128
Franklin Springs, GA 30639

Fort Wayne Bible College
1025 W. Rudisill Blvd.
Ft. Wayne, IN 46807

Grace Bible College
1011 Aldon St S.W.
Grand Rapids, MI 49509

Gulf Coast Bible College
911 W. 11th St.
Houston, TX 77008

Johnson Bible College
Kimberlin Heights, Rural Station
Knoxville, TN 37920

Kentucky Christian College
Grayson, Kentucky 41143

Emmaus Bible College
156 N. Oak Park Ave
Oak Park, IL 60301
(Applicant Institution)

L.I.F.E. Bible College
1100 Glendale Blvd.
Los Angeles, CA 90026

Lincoln Christian College
Box 178
Lincoln, IL 62656

Moody Bible Institute
820 N. La Salle St.
Chicago, IL 60610

Open Bible College
2633 Fleur Dr.
Des Moines, IA 50321

Philadelphia College of Bible
1800 Arch St.
Philadelphia, PA 19103

Reformed Bible College
1869 Robinson Road, S.E.
Grand Rapids, MI 49506

Southern Bible College
P.O. Box 9636
Houston, TX 77015

Southwestern Assemblies of God College
1200 Sycamore St.
Waxahachie, TX 75165

Valley Forge Christian College
Charlestown Road
Phoenixville, PA 19460

Washington Bible College
6511 Princess Garden Pkwy.
Lanham, MD 20801

Wesley College
P.O. Box 69
Florence, MS 39073

West Coast Bible College
6901 N. Maple St.
Fresno, CA 93710

Western Pentecostal Bible College
Box 1000
Clayburn, B.C. Canada VOX 1EO

The following entry is a listing for a typical Bible college:

Covington Bible Institute
Covington Theological Seminary, Inc.
P.O. Box #176
Rossville, Georgia 30741

2005 South Cedar Lane
Ft. Oglethorpe, Georgia

(404) 866-1316
(404) 866-5626

Background: Individually graded and self-paced pastoral training; founded in 1977, by Dr. H.D. Shuemake, as a nonprofit corporation. Located in Ft. Oglethorpe, Georgia.

Admissions: Open to all who have "accepted the Lord Jesus Christ as his or her Savior." Credits are accepted from other schools.

Tuition: Varies from $10 for a high school diploma to $600 for their Master's and Doctoral programs.

Degrees Offered: Varying from a Bachelor of Ministry to the Master of Religious Education to the Doctor of Sacred Theology.

Program:

Doctor of Sacred Theology Program (suggested)
Old Testament Studies   4 hours
New Testament Studies   4 hours
Apologetics   4 hours
Professional Guidance   8 hours
Thesis   16 hours

147

This is a fairly typical self-paced program. Incidentally, there are innumerable schools of this type, especially throughout the South, from which such degrees can be had. Their acceptability and validity will depend solely upon the individual and the circumstances under which he or she makes use of them. We certainly would not recommend presenting them as a credential to IBM, etc.

Law Schools

The next area of concern herein is the nontraditional pursuit of the law. The requirements for admission to the bar vary from state to state. Some jurisdictions require that you attend an accredited law school and pass the bar exam before you practice the law. Other states require that you graduate from an accredited law school, but do not require that you pass a bar exam.

There are considerable variations among the requirements for admission to the bar. California is, as usual, out in front on this point since it is the only state that allows you to study the law by correspondence. Consequently, the state is loaded with law schools, unaccredited and accredited, which can provide you a legal and legitimate means of studying the law. These institutions offer you an alternative means of studying law and becoming entitled to take the California bar exam. You would then first have to practice law for five years in California before you could transfer your law degree elsewhere, but this may be a viable alternative for some.

It was once the case that an individual apprenticed himself to an attorney and then took the bar exam in order to become a lawyer. *Although it is a method not commonly utilized,* the following states still allow for this procedure: Arkansas, California, Delaware, Georgia, Illinois, Kansas, Louisiana, Maine, Massachusetts, Mississippi, New York, North Carolina, North Dakota, Pennsylvania, Rhode Island, South Carolina, Texas, Vermont, Washington, and Virginia.

In other states you need not have a law degree from an accredited law school but must pass the bar exam instead: Alabama, Arizona, California, Colorado, Connecticut, Michigan, Mississippi, Nebraska, Ohio, Oklahoma, Tennessee, Vermont, Washington, and Wyoming.

Graduates from accredited law schools in the following states are lawyers upon graduation without a bar examination: Mississippi, Montana, South Dakota, West Virginia, and Wisconsin.

(One word of caution: Some of these alternative law schools appear to have a tendency to go out of business, a fact attested to by the large number of inquiries returned to the compiler of this book from defunct schools.)

Some law schools will require that you take the Law School Admissions Test to qualify for admission. Preparation material is available free of charge from:

**Educational Testing Service
P.O. Box #944—R
Princeton, New Jersey 08541**

For those of you who are about to expose yourselves to the LSAT, we recommend *Barron's How to Prepare for the Law School Admission Test.* It is well worth your money and time to work at learning how to take this test, or any test. While critics have raised serious doubts about the effectiveness of standardized testing, it is nonetheless a fact of modern life, and you *can* improve your score by learning test-taking strategies.

The Law School Data Assembly Service (LSDAS) serves as a collecting agency of college transcripts required for law-schools admissions offices. LSDAS analyzes undergraduate work, combines the analysis with LSAT scores, and supplies the resulting report to those schools you designate.

You may obtain a copy of the registration forms for the Law School Admissions Forms by writing to:

**Educational Testing Service
P.O. Box #955
Princeton, New Jersey 08540**

**Educational Testing Service
P.O. Box #1502
Berkeley, California 94701**

There is no point in going into great detail about the Law School Admission Test because the sample-test books such as Barron's mentioned above accomplish this task so well. You are well advised to visit a good bookstore and check their reference section for study- and exam-preparation guides. There are literally hundreds of these publications, and some of them can do you a great deal of good. Allow me to emphasize that you must buy new copies of such guides and not check dated ones out of a library. This is the only way you will get the most current information available.

The study of law may be accomplished through several processes. The *case system* involves the study and analysis of selected cases and classroom discussion of the rules of law established or illustrated by those cases. The problem method, seminars, written assignments, simulated exercises, and other methods and materials are also utilized. Research in a law library is a substantial part of the process of legal education.

First- and second-year law students will take some or all of the following courses:

Contracts	Legal Bibliography or Legal Method
Torts	Evidence
Criminal Law	Federal Income Tax
Property	Decedents' Estates
Constitutional Law	Agency and Partnership
Civil Procedure	Corporations

Third-year students, and some second-year students will take the following:

Professional Responsibility	Legislation
Estate and Gift Tax	Conflicts of Law
Equity	Federal Jurisdiction
Criminal Procedure	Appellate Advocacy
Trial Advocacy	Labor Law
Bankruptcy	Administrative Law
Domestic Relations	Corporate Taxation
Insurance	Damages
Local Government Law	

Medical Schools

The final portion of this discussion involves the study of medicine for those who have been unable to secure admission to a U.S. medical college. Those interested in foreign medical study should review the listing for St. George's University at the end of this section.

While it is possible to earn a medical degree abroad (generally in one of the less-developed or developing countries), there is increasing and considerable skepticism about the quality of such an education. At a time when there is an increasing glut of physicians on the U.S. health economy, coupled with the increasing use of highly qualified paramedics and physician's assistants, the would-be consumer of foreign medical education must be very, very careful, lest his or her time, effort, and money go for nought.

Those who decide to attend a foreign medical school because their age is a barrier to admission to a U.S. medical school *might* be in a better position than those who could not meet the academic standards in a U.S. school. There has been a toughening of standards in progress in recent years, but this fact does not imply that these foreign schools are "diploma mills" or that all those who attend are seeking an easy route to a medical degree. In fact, those who do attend these schools have considerable hurdles to overcome, culturally, linguistically, and hence, academically.

A number of foreign medical programs have been evaluated by:

The Educational Commission for Foreign Medical Graduates
3624 Market Street
Philadelphia, Pennsylvania 19104

The following is a list of several schools and information offices where a person can learn how to pursue a foreign medical education, though it is by no means complete, nor do these schools necessarily constitute the best of the foreign medical schools:

Universidad Cifas
Escuela de Medicina
P.O. Box 2549
Santo Domingo, Dominican Republic

U.S. Admissions Office
12820 Whittier Boulevard
Whittier, California 90602

(213) 696-4451

Saint Lucia Health Sciences University
Faculty of Medicine
Castries, St. Lucia, West Indies

St. Lucia Health Sciences University
1501 Sunbowl Drive
El Paso, Texas 79902

(915) 532-5848

American University of the Caribbean
School of Medicine
U.S. Office
100 N.W. 37th Avenue
Miami, Florida 33125

Kalmecac
Centro de Estudios Universitarios
Xochicalco
Apartado Postal 1377
Ensenada, B.C. Mexico

Telephone 4-09-52

C.E.U.X U.S. Office
P.O. Box #604
Chula Vista, California 92011

The following is a sample listing of one such foreign medical school:

St. George's University
School of Medicine
Foreign Medical School Services Corporation
1 East Main Street
Bay Shore, New York 11706

(516) 665-8600

Background: There is a stiff competition for the limited number of slots in American medical colleges. The result is that, as of December 1981 approximately 14,000 Americans are studying medicine abroad. This is compared to about 2000 in 1971, according to an article which appeared in *The Wall Street Journal* (December 21, 1981). Some students may not be academically qualified for American medical colleges, others are too old, and the Bakke case highlighted the admissions problems attending affirmative-action policies. But regardless of the reasons, the hazards of studying medicine abroad, i.e., not being admitted to practice medicine here in the U.S. after all of the work involved overseas, are increasing rapidly each year. Essentially, there is growing doubt in the medical community, and among regulators, that foreign trained physicians are not up to current American standards. This rather lengthy warning has been included lest any one be misled. Nonetheless, a proper part of a book such as this is a brief look at alternative medical education.

According to a study by the Educational Commission for Foreign Medical Graduates (ECFMG), St. George's University is among the top three foreign medical schools for alternative medical study. An evaluation of various foreign medical-school programs by ECFMG has been provided at the conclusion of this chapter.

Admission: "The Board of Admission takes many criteria into consideration including undergraduate and graduate performance, Medical College Admission Test scores, health professions experience, recommendations, and personal interviews."

Tuition:

Student per Semester Fees

Tuition Deposit	$ 500.00
Tuition Balance (January 1982)	$3325.00
Total Tuition (January 1982)	$3825.00
Tuition Balance (August 1982)	$3500.00
Total Tuition (August 1982)	$4000.00
Dormitory Fee	$ 650.00
Meal Plan Fee (January 1982)	$ 875.00
(August 1982)	$ 925.00
Books (approximately)	$ 175.00

Degrees Awarded: M.D.

Study Program: A four-year period of nine semesters which "provides extensive and rigorous training in the basic medical sciences and in the clinical disciplines." "The first two years of study, the first through fourth semesters of eighteen weeks each, are taken at St. George's University in Grenada and concentrate on the traditional basic science disciplines. These courses are taught by a full-time faculty augmented by visiting professors from medical schools in the United States and the United Kingdom." The fifth and sixth semesters consist of clinical clerkships in hospitals in St. Vincent, Grenada, and St. Kitts. "This experience exposes the students to the health care problems of tropical, less developed countries and, because of the absence of advanced medical technology, forces the students to rely heavily on history taking, physical examination, and clinical diagnosis." The seventh and eighth semesters are foreign externships at modern teaching hospitals. The ninth semester is an elective period for the pursuit of a specialty.

Credit for Life Experience: "Students matriculated within a medical school program listed with the World Health Organization qualify for transfer into the second through fifth semesters."

Time Required: Four years, nine semesters.

8
APPENDICES

Appendix A
Degrees Offered by Nontraditional Schools

A.A.	Associate of Arts
A.A.S.	Associate of Applied Science
A.S.E.	Associate of Science in Engineering
B.A.	Bachelor of Arts
B.B.A.	Bachelor of Business Administration
B.B.S.	Bachelor of Bible Studies
B.F.A.	Bachelor of Fine Arts
B.M.	Bachelor of Music
B.S.	Bachelor of Science
Th.B.	Bachelor of Theology
B.L.S.	Bachelor of Liberal Studies
B.R.E.	Bachelor of Religious Studies or Education
M.A.	Master of Arts
M.Ed.	Master of Education
Th.M.	Master of Theology
Min.M.	Master of Ministry
M.B.A.	Master of Business Education
M. Eng.	Master of Engineering
M.S.	Master of Science
M.F.A.	Master of Fine Arts
M.A.T.	Master of Arts in Teaching
M.L.S.	Master of Library Science
D.A.	Doctor of Administration
Ph.D.	Doctor of Philosophy
Ed.D.	Doctor of Education
Psy.D.	Doctor of Psychology
D.Sc.	Doctor of Science
D.D.	Doctor of Divinity
D.M.	Doctor of Ministry
D.A.	Doctor of Arts
D.B.A.	Doctor of Business Administration
D.F.A.	Doctor of Fine Arts
D.P.A.	Doctor of Public Administration
J.D.	Doctor of Jurisprudence
M.D.	Doctor of Medicine

Appendix B
Nationally Recognized Accrediting Agencies and Associations

The following regional and national accrediting agencies and associations have been recognized by the U.S. Secretary of Education as reliable authorities concerning the quality of education or training offered by educational institutions or programs. The dates included with each entry are: date of initial listing/date of action taken as result of last full-scale review/date of next regular review.

Regional Institutional Accrediting Associations

Connecticut, Maine, Massachusetts, New Hampshire, Rhode Island, Vermont
New England Association of Schools and Colleges
1976/1981
131 Middlesex Turnpike
Burlington, Massachusetts 01803
Tel. (617) 272-6450
Richard J. Bradley, Executive Director

Commissions:

Commission on Independent Schools
Ralph O. West, Director of Evaluation
(initially recognized in 1974)

Commission on Institutions of Higher Education
William J. MacLeod, Director of Evaluation
(initially recognized in 1952)

Commission on Public Schools
Robert J. O'Donnell, Director of Evaluation
(initially recognized in 1973)

Commission on Vocational, Technical, Career Institutions
Daniel S. Maloney, Director of Evaluation
(initially recognized in 1973)

Regional Institutional Accrediting Commissions

Alabama, Florida, Georgia, Kentucky, Louisiana, Mississippi, North Carolina, South Carolina, Tennessee, Texas, Virginia
Commission on Colleges
Southern Association of Colleges and Schools
1952/1979/1981

Gordon W. Sweet, Executive Director
795 Peachtree Street, N.E.
Atlanta, Georgia 30365
Tel. (404) 897-6125

Commission on Occupational Education Institutions
Southern Association of Colleges and Schools
1969/1977/1981
Bob E. Childers, Executive Director
795 Peachtree Street, N.E.
Atlanta, Georgia 30365
Tel. (404) 897-6164

Alaska, Idaho, Montana, Nevada, Oregon, Utah, Washington
Commission on Colleges
Northwest Association of Schools and Colleges
1952/1977/1981
James F. Bemis, Executive Director
3700-B University Way, N.E.
Seattle, Washington 98105
Tel. (206) 543-0195

Arizona, Arkansas, Colorado, Illinois, Indiana, Iowa, Kansas, Michigan, Minnesota, Missouri, Nebraska, New Mexico, North Dakota, Ohio, Oklahoma, South Dakota, West Virginia, Wisconsin, Wyoming
Commission on Institutions of Higher Education
North Central Association of Colleges and Schools
1952/1977/1981
Thurston E. Manning, Director
1221 University Avenue
Boulder, Colorado 80302
Tel. (800) 525-0840

Commission on Schools
North Central Association of Colleges and Schools
1974/1976/1981
John W. Vaughn, Executive Director
1221 University Avenue
Boulder, Colorado 80302
Tel. (800) 525-0840

California, Hawaii, the territory of Guam and such other areas of the Pacific Trust Territories as may apply to it
Accrediting Commission for Community and Junior Colleges
Western Association of Schools and Colleges
1952/1976/1981
Robert E. Swenson, Executive Director
9053 Soquel Drive
Aptos, California 95003
Tel. (408) 688-7575

Accrediting Commission for Schools
Western Association of Schools and Colleges
1974/1979/1983
Lyle Siverson, Executive Director
1614 Rollins Road
Burlingame, California 90410
Tel. (415) 697-7711

Accrediting Commission for Senior Colleges and Universities
Western Association of Schools and Colleges
1952/1976/1981
Kay J. Andersen, Executive Director
c/o Mills College, Box 9990
Oakland, California 94613
Tel. (415) 632-5000

Canal Zone, Delaware, District of Columbia, Maryland, New Jersey, New York, Pennsylvania, Puerto Rico, Virgin Islands
Commission on Higher Education
Middle States Association of Colleges and Schools
1952/1976/1981
Robert Kirkwood, Executive Director
3624 Market Street
Philadelphia, Pennsylvania 19104
Tel. (215) 662-5606

National Institutional and Specialized Accrediting Bodies

ALLIED HEALTH
Blood bank technologist
Cytotechnologist
Histologic technician
Medical assistant
Medical laboratory technician (certificate and associate degree)
Medical record administrator and medical record technician
Medical technologist
Nuclear medicine technologist
Occupational therapist

Physician's assistant (assistant to the primary care physician and surgeon's assistant)
Radiation therapy technologist and radiographer
Respiratory therapist and respiratory therapy technician
Surgical technologist ·
    Committee on Allied Health Education and Accreditation
American Medical Association
1952/1978/1982
John E. Beckley, Secretary
535 North Dearborn Street
Chicago, Illinois 60610
Tel. (312) 751-6272

The Committee on Allied Health Education and Accreditation of the American Medical Association is recognized as a coordinating agency for accreditation of education for the allied health occupations listed above. In carrying out its accreditation activities, CAHEA cooperates with the review committees sponsored by various allied health and medical specialty organizations. For information concerning the cooperating review committee and dates relative to Department of Education recognition and next review, refer to the disciplines as listed separately below. Other allied health disciplines accredited by agencies recognized by the Department outside the aegis of CAHEA are also listed below.

ARCHITECTURE
First professional-degree programs
    National Architectural Accrediting Board, Inc.
    1952/1976/1981
    Hugo G. Blasdel, Executive Director
    1735 New York Avenue, N.W.
    Washington, D.C. 20006
    Tel. (202) 783-2007

ART
Professional schools and programs
    Commission on Accreditation and Membership
    National Association of Schools of Art
    1966/1976/1981
    Samuel Hope, Executive Director
    11250 Roger Bacon Drive
    Suite 5
    Reston, Virginia 22090
    Tel. (703) 437-0700

BIBLE COLLEGE EDUCATION
Bible colleges and institutes

Commission on Accrediting
American Association of Bible Colleges
1952/1977/1981
John Mostert, Executive Director, AABC
Box 1523
Fayetteville, Arkansas 72701
Tel. (501) 521-8164

BLIND AND VISUALLY HANDICAPPED
EDUCATION
Specialized schools for the blind and visually handi-
capped
**National Accreditation Council for Agencies
Serving the Blind and Visually Handicapped**
1971/1976/1981
Richard W. Bleecker, Executive Director
79 Madison Avenue
New York, New York 10016
Tel. (212) 683-8581

BLOOD BANK TECHNOLOGY
Programs for the blood bank technologist
Committee on Allied Health Education and Ac-
creditation
American Medical Association
(See listing under ALLIED HEALTH, above)
In cooperation with the
Subcommittee on Accreditation
American Association of Blood Banks
1974/1978/1981
Lois James, Executive Director, AABB
1828 L Street, N.W., Suite 608
Washington, D.C. 20036
Tel. (202) 872-8333

BUSINESS
Baccalaureate and graduate degree programs in
business and management
Accreditation Council
**American Assembly of Collegiate Schools of
Business**
1952/1980/1982
William K. Laidlaw, Jr., Executive Vice Presi-
dent, AACSB
11500 Olive Street Road
St. Louis, Missouri 63141
Tel. (314) 872-8481

Private, postsecondary degree and non-degree granting institutions that are predominantly organized
to train students for business careers
Accrediting Commission
**Association of Independent Colleges and
Schools**
1956/1975/1981

James M. Phillips, Executive Director
1730 M Street, N.W.
Washington, D.C. 20036
Tel. (202) 659-2460

CHIROPRACTIC
Programs leading to the D.C. degree
Commission on Accreditation
The Council on Chiropractic Education
1974/1979/1982
Ralph G. Miller, Executive Secretary, CCE
3209 Ingersoll Avenue
Des Moines, Iowa 50312
Tel. (515) 255-2184

CLINICAL PASTORAL EDUCATION
Professional training centers
**Association for Clinical Pastoral Education,
Inc.**
1969/1976/1981
Charles E. Hall, Jr., Executive Director
Interchurch Center, Suite 450
475 Riverside Drive
New York, New York 10027
Tel. (212) 870-2558

CONTINUING EDUCATION
Programs in non-collegiate continuing education
Accrediting Commission
**Council for Non-Collegiate Continuing Edu-
cation**
1978/1981
Homer Kempfer
Executive Director
6 North Sixth Street
Richmond, Virginia 23219
Tel. (804) 648-6742

COSMETOLOGY
Cosmetology schools and programs
**National Accrediting Commission of Cos-
metology Arts and Sciences**
1970/1979/1982
Jerald W. Donaway, Executive Director
1735 K Street, N.W.
Washington, D.C. 20006
Tel. (202) 331-9550

CYTOTECHNOLOGY
Programs for the cytotechnologist
Committee on Allied Health Education and
Accreditation
American Medical Association
(See listing under ALLIED HEALTH, above)

In cooperation with the
    Cytotechnology Programs Review Committee
    American Society of Cytology
1974/1978/1982
Bernard Naylor, Chairman
Department of Pathology, Box 45
University of Michigan
Ann Arbor, Michigan 48109
Tel. (313) 763-4564

DANCE AND THEATER
Independent dance and theater institutions
    **Joint Commission on Dance and Theater Ac-
    creditation, which is sponsored by the Na-
    tional Association of Schools of Art and the
    National Association of Schools of Music**
1979/1982
Samuel Hope, Executive Director
11250 Roger Bacon Drive, No. 5
Reston, Virginia 22090
Tel. (703) 437-0700

DENTAL AND DENTAL AUXILIARY
PROGRAMS
Programs leading to the DDS or DMD degree, ad-
    vanced dental specialty programs, general prac-
    tice residency programs and programs in dental
    hygiene, dental assisting and dental technology
    Commission on Dental Accreditation
    American Dental Association
1952/1977/1981
Robert J. Pollock, Jr., Secretary
211 East Chicago Avenue
Chicago, Illinois 60611
Tel. (312) 440-2701

DIETETICS
Coordinated undergraduate programs in dietetics
    and dietetic internships
    Commission on Accreditation
    The American Dietetic Association
1974/1977/1981
Gloria Archer, Coordinator
430 North Michigan Avenue
Chicago, Illinois 60611
Tel. (312) 280-5000

ENGINEERING
First professional degree programs in engineering,
    graduate programs leading to advanced entry
    into the engineering profession, and associate
    and baccalaureate degree programs in engineer-
    ing technology
    **Accreditation Board for Engineering and
    Technology, Inc.**
1952/1977/1981

David R. Reyes-Guerra, Executive Director
345 East 47th Street
New York, New York 10017
Tel. (212) 644-7685

FORESTRY
Programs leading to a bachelor's or higher first pro-
    fessional degree, and related resource-oriented
    programs
    Society of American Foresters
1952/1977/1981
Ronald R. Christensen, Director of Professional
    Programs
5400 Grosvenor Lane
Washington, D.C. 20014
Tel. (301) 897-8720

FUNERAL SERVICE EDUCATION
Independent schools and collegiate departments
    Committee on Accreditation
    American Board of Funeral Service Education
1972/1976/1981
William H. Ford, Administrator, ABFSE
201 Columbia Street
Fairmont, West Virginia 26554
Tel. (304) 366-2403

HEALTH SERVICES ADMINISTRATION
Graduate programs in health services administra-
    tion
    **Accrediting Commission on Education for
    Health Services Administration**
1970/1978/1982
Gary L. Filerman, Executive Secretary
One Dupont Circle, N.W.
Washington, D.C. 20036
Tel. (202) 659-4354

HISTOLOGIC TECHNOLOGY
Programs for the histologic technician
    Committee on Allied Health Education and
    Accreditation
    American Medical Association
    (See listing under ALLIED HEALTH, above)
In cooperation with the
    **National Accrediting Agency for Clinical Lab-
    oratory Sciences, which is sponsored by the
    American Society for Medical Technology
    and the American Society of Clinical Pa-
    thologists**
1974/1978/1982
Carol Elkins, Executive Director
222 Riverside Plaza, Suite 1512
Chicago, Illinois 60606
Tel. (312) 648-0270

161

HOME STUDY EDUCATION
Home study schools
    Accrediting Commission
    National Home Study Council
    1959/1980/1984
    William A. Fowler, Executive Secretary
    1601 18th Street, N.W.
    Washington, D.C. 20009
    Tel. (202) 234-5100

INTERIOR DESIGN EDUCATION
Professional and technical programs
    Committee on Accreditation
    Foundation for Interior Design Education Research
    1975/1979/1983
    Edna V. Kane, Director of Administration, FIDER
    730 Fifth Avenue
    New York, New York 10019
    Tel. (212) 586-7266

JOURNALISM
First professional degree programs
    Accrediting Committee
    American Council on Education for Journalism
    1952/1976/1981
    Baskett Mosse, Executive Secretary
    563 Essex Court
    Deerfield, Illinois 60015
    Tel. (312) 948-5840

LANDSCAPE ARCHITECTURE
First professional degree programs
    Landscape Architectural Accreditation Board
    American Society of Landscape Architects
    1971/1977/1981
    Samuel Miller, Director
    Education and Research, ASLA
    1900 M Street, N.W., Suite 750
    Washington, D.C. 20036
    Tel. (202) 466-7730

LAW
Professional schools
    Council of the Section of Legal Education and Admissions to the Bar
    American Bar Association
    1952/1979/1982
    James F. White
    Consultant on Legal Education, ABA
    Indiana University
    735 West New York Street
    Indianapolis, Indiana 46202
    Tel. (317) 264-8071

LIBRARIANSHIP
    Graduate programs leading to the first profes-
        sional degree
    Committee on Accreditation
    American Library Association
    1952/1977/1981
    Elinor Yungmeyer, Accreditation Officer
    50 East Huron Street
    Chicago, Illinois 60611
    Tel. (312) 944-6780

MARRIAGE AND FAMILY THERAPY
Graduate degree programs and clinical training
    programs
    Commission on Accreditation for Marriage and
        Family Therapy Education
    American Association for Marriage and Family Therapy
    1978/1980/1983
    John Shalett, Executive Director
    924 West Ninth Street
    Upland, California 91786
    Tel. (714) 981-0888

MEDICAL ASSISTANT EDUCATION
Private medical assistant schools and programs
    Accrediting Bureau of Health Education Schools
    1974/1980/1984
    Hugh A. Woosley, Administrator
    Oak Manor Offices, 29089 U.S. 20 West
    Elkhart, Indiana 46514
    Tel. (219) 293-0124

One- and two-year medical assistant programs
    Committee on Allied Health Education and Ac-
        creditation
    American Medical Association
    (See listing under ALLIED HEALTH, above)
In cooperation with the
    Curriculum Review Board
    American Association of Medical Assistants
    1974/1976/1981
    Ina Yenerich, Executive Director, AAMA
    One East Wacker Drive, Suite 2110
    Chicago, Illinois 60601
    Tel. (312) 944-2722

MEDICAL LABORATORY TECHNICIAN
EDUCATION
Schools and programs for the medical laboratory
    technician
    Accrediting Bureau of Health Education Schools
    1969/1980/1984

162

(See listing under MEDICAL ASSISTANT EDUCATION, above)
Associate degree and certificate programs for the medical laboratory technician

Committee on Allied Health Education and Accreditation
American Medical Association
(See listing under ALLIED HEALTH, above)

In cooperation with the

National Accrediting Agency for Clinical Laboratory Sciences
1974/1978/1982
(See listing under HISTOLOGIC TECHNOLOGY, above)

MEDICAL RECORD EDUCATION
Programs for the medical record administrator and medical record technician

Committee on Allied Health Education and Accreditation
American Medical Association
(See listing under ALLIED HEALTH, above)

In cooperation with the

Council on Education
American Medical Record Association
1952/1978/1982
Laura Anne Biglow
Director, Academic Department, AMRA
874 North Michigan Avenue, Suite 1850
John Hancock Center
Chicago, Illinois 60611
Tel. (312) 787-2672

MEDICAL TECHNOLOGY
Professional programs

Committee on Allied Health Education and Accreditation
American Medical Association
(See listing under ALLIED HEALTH, above)

In cooperation with the

National Accrediting Agency for Clinical Laboratory Sciences
1952/1978/1982
(See listing under HISTOLOGIC TECHNOLOGY, above)

MEDICINE
Programs leading to the M.D. degree

Liaison Committee on Medical Education of the Council on Medical Education of the American Medical Association and the Executive Council of the Association of American Medical Colleges
1952/1980/1984

The LCME is administered in odd-numbered years, beginning each July 1, by:
Edward S. Petersen, Secretary, LCME
American Medical Association
535 North Dearborn Street
Chicago, Illinois 60610
Tel. (312) 751-6310

The LCME is administered in even-numbered years, beginning each July 1, by:
J. R. Schofield, Secretary, LCME
Association of American Medical Colleges
One Dupont Circle, N.W., Suite 200
Washington, D.C. 20036
Tel. (202) 828-0670

MICROBIOLOGY
Postdoctoral programs

Committee on Postdoctoral Educational Programs
American Academy of Microbiology
1979/1983
Robert D. Watkins, Administrative Coordinator
1913 I Street, N.W.
Washington, D.C. 20006
Tel. (202) 833-9680

MUSIC
Baccalaureate and graduate degree programs and non-degree granting institutions offering music education

National Association of Schools of Music
1952/1977/1981
Samuel Hope, Executive Director
11250 Roger Bacon Drive, No. 5
Reston, Virginia 22090
Tel. (703) 437-0700

NUCLEAR MEDICINE TECHNOLOGY
Programs for the nuclear medicine technologist

Committee on Allied Health Education and Accreditation
American Medical Association
(See listing under ALLIED HEALTH, above)

In cooperation with the

Joint Review Committee on Educational Programs in Nuclear Medicine Technology, which is sponsored by the American College of Radiology, American Society of Clinical Pathologists, American Society for Medical Technology, American Society of Radiologic Technologists and the Society of Nuclear Medicine
1974/1978/1982

163

Elaine Cuklanz, Chairperson
445 S. 300 East
Salt Lake City, Utah 84111
Tel. (801) 355-9628

NURSING
Professional schools/programs of nurse anesthesia
　Council on Accreditation of Nurse Anesthesia
　　Schools/Programs
　American Association of Nurse Anesthetists
　1955/1976/1981
　Mary M. Cavagnaro, Executive Secretary
　216 Higgins Road
　Park Ridge, Illinois 60068
　Tel. (312) 692-7050

Practical nurse programs
　Accrediting Review Board
　National Association for Practical Nurse Education and Service, Inc.
　1967/1976/1981
　Lucille L. Etheridge, Executive Director, NAPNES
　254 West 31st Street
　New York, New York 10001
　Tel. (212) 736-4540

Professional, technical and practical nurse programs
　Board of Review for Baccalaureate and Higher
　　Degree Programs
　Board of Review for Diploma Programs
　Board of Review for Practical Nursing Programs
　Board of Review for Associate Degree Programs
　National League for Nursing, Inc.
　1952/1979/1983
　Margaret E. Walsh, Executive Director and
　　Secretary, NLN
　10 Columbus Circle
　New York, New York 10019
　Tel. (212) 582-1022

OCCUPATIONAL THERAPY
Professional programs
　Committee on Allied Health Education and
　　Accreditation
　American Medical Association
　(See listing under ALLIED HEALTH, above)
In cooperation with the
　Accreditation Committee
　American Occupational Therapy Association
　1952/1978/1982
　Martha Kirkland, Coordinator, Accreditation

1383 Picard Drive
Rockville, Maryland 20850
Tel. (301) 948-9626

OCCUPATIONAL, TRADE AND TECHNICAL EDUCATION
Private trade and technical schools
　Accrediting Commission
　National Association of Trade and Technical Schools
　1967/1979/1983
　William A. Goddard, Secretary
　2021 K Street, N.W., Room 350
　Washington, D.C. 20036
　Tel. (202) 296-8892

OPTOMETRY
Professional programs
　Council on Optometric Education
　American Optometric Association
　1952/1977/1981
　Brian Andrew, Executive Secretary
　243 North Lindbergh Boulevard
　St. Louis, Missouri 63141
　Tel. (314) 991-4100

OSTEOPATHIC MEDICINE
Programs leading to the D.O. degree
　American Osteopathic Association
　1952/1979/1983
　William Douglas Ward, Director
　Office of Osteopathic Education
　212 East Ohio Street
　Chicago, Illinois 60611
　Tel. (312) 280-5800

PHARMACY
Professional degree programs
　American Council on Pharmaceutical Education
　1952/1978/1982
　Daniel A. Nona, Executive Director
　One East Wacker Drive
　Chicago, Illinois 60601
　Tel. (312) 467-6222

PHYSICAL THERAPY
Professional programs for the physical therapist
　and programs for the physical therapist assistant
　Committee on Accreditation in Education
　American Physical Therapy Association*
　1977/1980/1984
　James R. Clinkingbeard, Director
　Department of Education Affairs, APTA

164

1156 15th Street, N.W.
Washington, D.C. 20005
Tel. (202) 466-2070

*Previously recognized in collaboration with the American Medical Association, 1952-1976.

PHYSICIAN'S ASSISTANT EDUCATION
Programs for the assistant to the primary care physician and the surgeon's assistant
Committee on Allied Health Education and Accreditation
American Medical Association
(See listing under ALLIED HEALTH, above)
In cooperation with the
Joint Review Committee on Education Programs for Physician's Assistants, which is sponsored by the American Academy of Family Physicians, American Academy of Pediatrics, American Academy of Physician's Assistants, American College of Physicians, American College of Surgeons, American Society of Internal Medicine, and the Association for Physician Assistant Programs
1974/1978/1982
Robert B. Chevalier
St. Francis Hospital
Beech Grove, Indiana 46107
Tel. (317) 783-8137

PODIATRY
Colleges of podiatric medicine, including professional and graduate degree programs
Council on Podiatry Education
American Podiatry Association
1952/1979/1982
Warren G. Ball, Director
20 Chevy Chase Circle, N.W.
Washington, D.C. 20015
Tel. (202) 537-4970

PSYCHOLOGY
Doctoral and internship programs in clinical, counseling and school psychology and doctoral programs in professional psychology
Committee on Accreditation
American Psychological Association
1970/1979/1981
Meredith P. Crawford, Administrative Officer for Accreditation, APA
1200 17th Street, N.W.
Washington, D.C. 20036
Tel. (202) 833-7692

PUBLIC HEALTH
Graduate school of public health and graduate programs offered outside schools of public health in community health education and in community health/preventive medicine
Council on Education for Public Health
1974/1977/1981
Janet A. Strauss, Executive Director
1015 15th Street, N.W.
Washington, D.C. 20005
Tel. (202) 789-1050

RABBINICAL AND TALMUDIC EDUCATION
Rabbinical and Talmudic schools
Accreditation Commission
Association of Advanced Rabbinical and Talmudic Schools
1974/1977/1981
Bernard Fryshman, Executive Director
175 Fifth Avenue, Room 711
New York, New York 10010
Tel. (212) 477-0950

RADIOLOGIC TECHNOLOGY
Programs for the radiographer and radiation therapy technologist
Committee on Allied Health Education and Association
American Medical Association
(See listing under ALLIED HEALTH, above)
In cooperation with the
Joint Review Committee on Education in Radiologic Technology, which is sponsored by the American College of Radiology and the American Society of Radiologic Technologists
1957/1978/1982
Robert L. Coyle, Executive Director
307 North Michigan Avenue, Suite 1801
Chicago, Illinois 60601
Tel. (312) 726-9150

RESPIRATORY THERAPY
Programs for the respiratory therapist and respiratory therapy technician
Committee on Allied Health Education and Accreditation
American Medical Association
(See listing under ALLIED HEALTH, above)
In cooperation with the
Joint Review Committee for Respiratory Therapy Education, which is sponsored by the American Association for Respiratory Therapy, American College of Chest Physicians,

165

American Society of Anesthesiologists and the American Thoracic Society
1974/1978/1982
Philip A. von der Heydt
Executive Director
1701 West Euless Boulevard
Euless, Texas 76039
Tel. (817) 283-2835

SOCIAL WORK
Master's and baccalaureate degree programs
Commission on Accreditation
Council on Social Work Education
1952/1976/1981
Sidney Berengarten, Director
Division of Standards and Accreditation, CSWE
111 Eighth Avenue, Suite 501
New York, New York 10011
Tel. (212) 697-0467

SPEECH-LANGUAGE PATHOLOGY AND AUDIOLOGY
Master's degree programs
Council on Professional Standards in Speech-Language Pathology and Audiology
American Speech-Language-Hearing Association
1967/1980/1984
Billie Ackerman, Assistant Director
Educational Scientific Programs
10801 Rockville Pike
Rockville, Maryland 20852
Tel. (301) 897-5700

SURGICAL TECHNOLOGY
Programs for the surgical technologist
Committee on Allied Health Education and Accreditation
American Medical Association
(See listing under ALLIED HEALTH, above)
In cooperation with the
Joint Review Committee on Education for the Surgical Technologist, which is sponsored by the American College of Surgeons, American Hospital Association, and the Association of Surgical Technologists
1978/1981
Sandra L. Wilkins
Secretary-Treasurer
Caller No. E
Littleton, Colorado 80120
Tel. (303) 978-9010

TEACHER EDUCATION
Baccalaureate and graduate degree programs
National Council for Accreditation of Teacher Education
1952/1979/1983
Lyn Gubser, Director
1919 Pennsylvania Avenue, N.W., Room 202
Washington, D.C. 20006
Tel. (202) 466-7496

THEOLOGY
Graduate professional degree programs offered by schools of theology
Commission on Accrediting
Association of Theological Schools in the United States and Canada
1952/1977/1981
Leon Pacala, Executive Director, ATS
Post Office Box 130
Vandalia, Ohio 45377
Tel. (513) 898-4654

VETERINARY MEDICINE
Programs leading to the DVM or VMD degrees and two-year programs for animal technicians
Council on Education
American Veterinary Medical Association
1952/1979/1983
Committee on Animal Technician Activities and Training
American Veterinary Medical Association
1977/1978/1982
R. Leland West, Director
Scientific Activities, AVMA
930 North Meacham Road
Schaumburg, Illinois 60196
Tel. (312) 885-8070

Other:
Registration [accreditation] of collegiate degree-granting programs or curriculums offered by institutions of higher education

New York State Board of Regents
1952/1980/1984
Gordon M. Ambach, Commissioner of Education
State Education Department

The University of the State of New York
Albany, New York 12224
Tel. (518) 457-3000

166

Appendix C
The State of California and Nontraditional Education

California has been quite progressive with regard to private, nontraditional, postsecondary education and enacted the Private Postsecondary Act of 1977 to foster diversity in the educational process. The "legislative intent" of the law is to "encourage privately supported education and protect the integrity of degrees and diplomas conferred by privately supported as well as publicly supported educational institutions."

These private schools, colleges, and/or universities are *legally authorized* to award diplomas, *provided* they meet the established criteria of the California State Department of Education's administrative code, which implements the various provisions of the law. Such legally authorized schools and colleges may or may not be *accredited,* which quite frequently has little or nothing to do with the actual quality of the institution's programs.

This legislation also protects the "consumer" of private education (which of course is frequently nontraditional education). This legislation and its administrative provisions are quite detailed and would not be of interest in their entirety to most readers of this guide. A complete copy of the legislation and administrative rules may be obtained by writing to the following address:

Office of Private Postsecondary Education
721 Capitol Mall
Sacramento, California 95814

Here are some of the major points of this law and its rules:
" 'Postsecondary educational institution' or 'institution' includes, but is not limited to, an academic, vocational, technical, business, professional, home study school, college, or university, or other organization (comprised of a person, firm, association, partnership, or corporation) which offers educational degrees or diplomas, or offers instruction or educational services primarily to persons who have completed or terminated their secondary education or who are beyond the age of compulsory high school attendance."

To protect against the possibility of such institutions turning into diploma mills, the administrative code stipulates that: "An institution shall not grant diplomas or degrees solely on the basis of education taken at, or credit transferred from, another institution or institutions, or *solely* on noninstructional learning experiences. An institution must provide instruction as a part of its program." Obviously this provision is a solid contribution to the credibility of these degrees. Other provisions of the regulations also deal with issues such as "honorary" degrees, the content of diplomas and degrees, and the manner in which records are to be maintained.

" 'Accredited' means that an institution has been recognized or approved as meeting the standards established by an accrediting agency recognized by the federal Department of Education or the Committee of Bar Examiners for the State of California." Institutions recognized by the Western Association of Schools and Colleges are also accredited. Accreditation is not extended to schools that have applied for it or that are provisionally accredited.

The legislation and regulations also contain stiff provisions to protect the consumer from fraud and to provide for a grievance process. Provisions are also made for a Student Tuition Recovery Fund, "for the purpose of relieving or mitigating pecuniary losses suffered by any *California resident* who is a student of an approved or authorized institution which charges prepaid tuition, as a result of such institution ceasing its operation for any reason." This type of information is provided to the student by the institution to comply with the requirements of the law.

There are numerous other provisions in this law and its accompanying regulations that provide definitions or stipulate requirements for state approval to operate but they will not be of interest to most readers and have not been reprinted in full.

INDEX